TEN HANDS FOR GOD

The Upper Room
Nashville, Tennessee

Ten Hands for God

First Printing: November, 1982 (5)
Library of Congress Catalog Card Number: 82–50947

ISBN 0–8358–0449–6

Printed in the United States of America

Contents

Preface 7
Introduction 9
Antone Tarazi—*Jerusalem* 13
Toshihiro Takami—*Japan* 27
Esther Park—*Hawaii* 41
Frank Field—*England* 49
Alain Rocourt—*Haiti* 61
Conclusion 77

Preface

Ten Hands for God is a needed book. There is an old adage that Christianity is not so much taught as caught. That generality has the weakness of all generalities, but it also possesses a kernel of truth. We Christians must demonstrate that we are redeemed before others will believe in our Redeemer.

The most powerful witness is a living model, and that is what this book is all about. I do not know anyone who could have written it better than my friend, Harry Haines. Harry has traveled the world all his life as a minister, serving first as a missionary, and for the last thirty years as the director of some of the most bold and exciting mission endeavors of the church.

He has selected five persons whose lives tell the story of the Christian life in a vivid way. These are heroes, and the world is in short supply of genuine heroes.

They are the kind of heroes to whom the church should look as models and witnesses. A saint is a Christian in full degree, and that is the life to which we are all called. In the best sense of the word, these people are saints.

Ten Hands for God is a book you will enjoy, but one which will challenge and call you to deeper commitment. I thank Harry Haines for sharing these stories with us. I thank God for these "ten hands for God" who are calls to me.

MAXIE D. DUNNAM

Introduction

This is a book about five people who have never met each other. They represent five different nationalities and not all speak a common language. If they ever did meet, they would be surprised to be told that they are very special people. What they have in common is a deep personal commitment to Jesus Christ and a strong belief that one person plus God is always in the majority. In Psalm 18:29, the psalmist speaks of the power of a resolute trust in God in the face of the impossible. "By my God I can leap over a wall."

Much effort in the lives of these five people has been spent in leaping over walls of discouragement, of disappointment, of overwhelming human need. Sometimes quite unknown to them, they have inspired many other people to leap over a wall and to attempt the impossible. They are all friends of mine of many years. They live in Nishinasuno, Japan; Honolulu, Hawaii; Jerusalem, West Bank; Port-au-Prince, Haiti; and Polegate, England.

During the last fifteen years I have had the rare privilege of traveling more than a million miles through ninety-two countries. I traveled not as a global jet-setter but on behalf of the ecumenical movement, representing the World Council of Churches for three years, Church World Service, the diaconal arm of the National Council of Churches, United States, and for the last sixteen years, the United Methodist Church. Only after eleven visits to India did I manage to see the Taj Mahal for an hour or so. I keep promising myself that some day I am going to book a plane ticket as a tourist to one of those beautiful, exotic places promoted by enterprising travel agents.

When I look at a world map, I no longer identify each country by historic landmarks, beautiful scenery, or wonderful hotels; instead, I think of people. I think of Chungking, the wartime capital of China. I remember Bishop W. Y. Chen, an amazing man of God whose life touched so many. Kuala Lumpur, Malaysia, will forever be identified in my thinking with many wonderful people like Dr. Soo Kim Lan, the first Malaysian Chinese woman ever to qualify as a western-trained doctor. New Delhi, India, brings to mind Bob Marble, an extraordinary missionary; Cairo, Egypt, the Reverend Samuel Habib, a devoted Coptic Evangelical clergyman; Geneva, Switzerland, Dr. Leslie Cook, preacher par excellence; Chimaltenango, Guatemala, Dr. Carroll Behrhorst, a physician in the Albert Schweitzer tradition. The list could go on country after country.

Why, then, out of this countless number have I selected these particular five persons? It is not easy, believe me; I could have included many more. One of these friends of many years, who out of almost total obscurity became front page news in the media and received the Nobel Peace Prize, is Mother Teresa, who said on my last visit to her in Calcutta, "You know, we all have a chance to do something beautiful for our God." These five and so many others have done something for our God, and their stories are worth recording to inspire others to go and do likewise.

I have called this book *Ten Hands for God* for two reasons. As I travel across the United States, I speak almost every Sunday in a different pulpit. In the conversations that often follow, I can almost guarantee that one person will come up to me and say in one form or another, "Yes, I know out there is the great world of suffering and hunger. I wish I could do something about it, but what can I do? I'm only one person." This book is about five people whose response to the great mountain of human need was, "I believe in miracles. By my God I can leap over a wall." Therefore, this book is a personal message to you to say if they can do it, you can. You can be part of God's answer. The other reason is that saints are in very short supply these days. One little boy stood in a great cathedral somewhat awed by the magnificent stained-glass windows of biblical and historical persons. He asked his mother in a very quiet voice, "Who are these?" He was told they are saints. His reply: "I see. A saint is someone who lets the light shine through." By that definition, these five qualify. To have known them, worked with some of them for various lengths of time, is to see the light of God shine through them, and my own life has been richer for it.

I write this introduction in the Pocono Mountains at Hemlock Farms. Outside, it is one degree Celsius, and fifteen inches of snow are on the ground. I know it's that deep because I have spent most of this morning shoveling a path to the woodpile that I stacked on a summer day last year. The complete silence is disturbed only by the crackling of a pine log on the blazing fire. I am thinking not only about these five people whose brief stories I want to share, but of an endless line of splendor, of the many people in so many different places whose friendship and shared experiences have touched my life, enriching, uplifting, and blessing it.

J. HARRY HAINES
January, 1983

Dr. Antone Tarazi

Great Talents Dedicated to Service

Jesus healed many who were sick with all kinds of diseases.
—Mark 1:34 (TEV)

The ancient Jews spoke of Jerusalem as the center of the world. Today the hopes and fears of millions of people—Jewish, Moslem, and Christian—revolve around this holiest of all cities where the three monotheistic faiths draw inspiration and life. Pilgrims to the Holy Land invariably find their way to the Mount of Olives where our Lord once stood and looked down on the city. It is reported he wept in anguish over the city that was soon to reject him.

Close to the traditional site where Jesus stood is the Makassed Hospital, dedicated to a healing ministry for the Palestinians who live along the West Bank. Among its dedicated team of doctors and nurses is Dr. Antone Tarazi, the only neurosurgeon for the eight hundred thousand Palestinians in the area.

Dr. Tarazi and his wife Rima Nasser Tarazi have spent their last fifteen years as part of the church's witness in one of the most turbulent areas in the world. It is a great tragedy that annually tens of thousands of Christian pilgrims go from the United States to walk where Jesus walked, to visit the places associated with the Bible, and then return home almost completely unaware of the existence of a great Arab Christian community in the Middle East, numbering at least nine million. In the last ten years, fifty thousand Palestinian Christians have left their West Bank homes and migrated to the West, perhaps never to return. The remaining fifty thousand share with their Moslem neighbors a deepening concern for their future.

Dr. Tarazi has elected not to leave Jerusalem despite the many tempting offers sent from America and Canada to this highly skilled, dedicated neurosurgeon. We sat together drinking black Turkish coffee in his office shortly after he had concluded a five-hour operation on a farmer who had been brought in with a malignant tumor of the brain. From where we sat we could see one of the most spectacular views in the world. We looked out across the olive groves on the Mount of Olives and then down the valley to the Garden of Gethsemane. We could just catch a glimpse of the onion-shaped domes of the Russian Orthodox church and beyond it the Church of All Nations. Then, as we looked across the Kedron Valley, in all its glory shone the great gold dome of the mosque of Omar; to the right of it the Church of the Holy Sepulchre in the old city of Jerusalem.

"It seems," said Dr. Tarazi, as I commented on this superb panorama, "that every stone here in this city is tinged with history. So many conquering armies have swept through the city since the time of our Lord. This city is my home, the place where God has called me to exercise my work as a physician and surgeon to help my people."

He talked at length about his work and the many long years of preparation for the tasks that he now performs daily in his hospital. He spoke with regret because at present his work was so shorthanded, and he sometimes felt despair.

Then he smiled and said, "You know, I never give up, because this ministry of healing is God's work. When I have done everything humanly possible to save another life, then the healing hand of our Christ must continue the work in that person's body and restore it again to fullness of health. I am a partner with our Lord whose ministry of healing was carried out in this very city so long ago." Then he shook his head and said, "You know, at the moment I have a nine- to twelve-months' backlog on neurosurgery. I get very worried at times because I feel that we must do so much more than we are doing now."

He described the operation he had just finished a short time before.

"Whenever I am ready for an operation, as I take the knife in my gloved hand, I bow my head and say one word in Arabic: *bismillah*, 'In the name of God.' Then I pause to ask God's guiding hand to work with me in what is the most delicate kind of operation that any doctor can perform. You literally have the life of your patient in your hands during the operation.

"For me, treating a sick person is a challenge. The illness must be conquered. A bad outcome of an operation is not acceptable to me, not what God wants. In the very worst situations sometimes my Moslem colleagues say,

 'This is destiny. It is the will of God.' But I'm not a fatalist. I don't accept that. To me a bad outcome of an operation is the result of a shortcoming in medical procedures which must be evaluated again and again until the correct answer is found and better surgery is used. I never cease to marvel at the amazing composition of the human body. It certainly is true to say, 'We are fearfully and wonderfully made.' I think that every Christian ought to study biology. The survival of the human race has a proven set of rules. The human race has survived irrespective of all the hardships it has encountered, and it has survived when modern medicine did not exist.

"The human being survives under terrible hardships because of very specific biological rules that control the body. For instance, when someone suffers from internal bleeding, many mechanisms within the human body automatically start to function to stop that bleeding. Those who succumb to internal bleeding are the ones in whom this defense mechanism to stop the bleeding has been exhausted. As soon as an ulcer starts bleeding, the clotting mechanism starts functioning. The stress factor comes into play to facilitate clotting. The stress reaction for that human being is to fight and defend itself. This is one of the big accomplishments in the history of surgery. We discover what goes into effect when the patient undergoes major trauma or is subject to a major operation similar to the one I performed a little while ago. The stress reaction is a normal biological reaction coming into play. I find myself again and again in this hospital standing back in utter amazement at the mystery of life. We doctors, armed as we are with the very finest of available knowledge, come up against this mystery and realize there is so much that we simply do not yet understand.

"I think a great analogy exists between my work as a surgeon, my constant probing into the way that the human body reacts biologically, and the reality of our material and political life around us. Our Lord said, 'I will build my church, and the powers of death shall not prevail against it' (Matt. 16:18). To me this means that the church as the family of God's people is God's representative on earth, and nothing can come our way to destroy this church. It has gone on for these last 1,900 years, seeking with all of its inadequacies to witness to the living power of God. I'm glad I am a doctor. It's a great privilege to bring hope. The persons who come here often despair of their own possibility of extension of their lives. I feel very sad as I see so many of my own Palestinian Christian neighbors leaving this area. Perhaps before very long, even the town of Bethlehem, sacred to us all, may for the first time lose most of its Christians as they migrate to the West."

As I talked with Dr. Tarazi, I was not surprised to find that his concern as a surgeon mingles with his concern for the existence of his own people along the West Bank and the Gaza. In this great city where people greet each other on the street, saying *salaam aleikum*, "peace be upon you," there is very little peace these days. As we talked further together, we took a step back to the beginning of the life of this amazing Christian who feels such deep pain and agony for his people and the work that God has called him to do.

For him, it all began when he was born in one of the oldest cities of the world, Gaza, located at the crossroads of the Middle East on the land bridge between northern Africa, Asia, and Europe, its shores washed by the Mediterranean Sea. Gaza has almost from the dawn of time witnessed the endless marching of alien armies through its streets and orange groves: Egyptian, Persian, Roman, Assyrian, Turkish, and in more recent times, British forces. Today, the city lies under military occupation of the state of Israel, and its future is debated endlessly in the halls of the United Nations.

Antone Tarazi was born into a family of seven children at the time of the British mandate when the Gaza Strip was known as Palestine. His father was a representative of the Shell Oil Company, and the family lived in a beautiful citrus grove close to the seashore. The first seventeen years of his life were relatively tranquil. This town of twenty-five thousand was predominantly Moslem, but there was a small Christian community, predominantly Greek Orthodox. His earliest recollections were of being taken weekly with his brothers and sisters to the church with its beautiful icons, the observation of the endless saints' days, and the high holy days of the Christian community.

Gaza today is a strip of land twenty-seven miles long and six miles wide, with a population of nearly five hundred thousand including the nearby refugee camps. The Tarazi family has always lived in the Gaza Strip, and they have always been part of the small Christian community. His father was the lay leader of the congregation. Antone himself sang in a choir as a child, and these were good times for his family. The priest of the congregation came from Bethlehem, good relationships existed between Moslems and Christians. "We never felt we were a minority. When the Moslem neighbors observed Ramadan, the fasting month, we didn't fast, but we enjoyed going to our Moslem neighbors' homes in the evening when the fast for the day had ended. There was endless eating and entertaining among our people. I studied the Koran with my Moslem school friends and found it very stimulating. As the sacred book of the Moslems, it has had a profound influence on the Arabic language.

"The British administration was in our town as a fact of life. It wasn't really oppressive, but they were aliens. We simply went about our own lives hoping the day would come when we would be allowed to decide our own destiny. My parents had lived under the Turkish government, then the British, today the Israeli administration, and tomorrow we really don't know. We are Palestinians, and we want to have the same rights for ourselves as we know other people around us have.

"I worked my way through high school at one of my father's gas stations. The day came when it was time to leave Gaza and go to the Arab school in Jerusalem. I had done well in school but never thought of being a doctor. It was just assumed by my family that I would go to Jerusalem and study, perhaps to be a teacher. Then it would be necessary to leave the country as there was no university for Arab students in our area. This meant going to Beirut, Lebanon, where I knew the American University, related to American churches, was there to help our people.

"Beirut, Lebanon, was a wonder city to me, coming from the little town of Gaza. For the next eight years this was to be my home. I experienced great kindness and understanding at the university. I was one of the privileged ones who, having gained entrance to the university, felt that my responsibility now was to become a responsible person to help my people. I think it was my early interest in the mystery of life and the study of biology in high school that led me to the decision to become a doctor. I don't know when I got my intuition or feeling to be a doctor. Indeed, at one time I was interested in engineering, and then I decided to go into human engineering. I can't say, 'God called me to be a doctor.' I just felt called to be a help to my people.

"I received my M.D. in 1952. Then, because of strong ties to the university in the United States, it seemed only natural that I should go to the United States to further my medical education. American University in Beirut had a special relationship with Princeton, but I decided to try Duke. When I arrived on the campus I felt welcome, and I saw a chance to further my training. I came in contact with a neurosurgeon during the eighteen months that I studied surgery. This was a brand-new field of surgery as far as I was concerned and was not available in Beirut or in my part of the Middle East. I said to myself, my people need this kind of help. I must specialize in it.

"While at Duke I came in contact for the first time with Protestant Christianity. It was all very different from anything I had known in the Gaza, and I was attracted to the weekly chapel services. I must tell you that being a Greek Orthodox is really a whole way of life. The church penetrates every part of your life. In a sense I guess I could say I was born into the church. We had always been there. It really didn't depend on the effective leadership of the priest. It depended on all the people together. From the earliest days I learned the need of prayer and of individual meditation. When I often went into the chapel at Duke it seemed natural to simply kneel there and ask God to direct my life.

"The internship in surgery at Duke was rotational. I worked along for a while in plastic surgery, orthopedic surgery, general surgery, and at that point I became fascinated with brain surgery. I went to the chief neurosurgeon and asked to be taken on as one of his special students. I was turned down. Why wasn't I selected? The chief neurosurgeon said, 'This is a new field, and it is given first to American students.' That is where it might have ended, but I refused to take a no. I asked, 'If you are not willing to train me, where is there an outstanding neurosurgeon anywhere on this continent who is internationally minded and not regionally minded?' In a sense, the doctor at Duke opened the door for me. He told me that I should apply to Dr. Wilder Penfield at McGill University in Montreal, Canada. I wrote, saying, 'I am an Arab from the Middle East, and I want to study with you. My people need this kind of help.' I went to McGill, and my five-year apprenticeship began. It seemed to me I was working day and night in that great university medical center.

"Life was a lot more tranquil at McGill than at Duke. After a year there, it seemed only right according to the tradition of my people that I should go home for a short visit, get married, and then return to my internship. I really didn't know my wife Rima before I married her. It was arranged. One of my cousins had met Rima Nasser, who was a music student and the daughter of a distinguished cabinet minister in the government of Jordan. Dr. Nasser was at the time the Minister of Foreign Affairs and lived in the town of Beir Zeit. This distinguished family of political and educational leaders were Episcopalians, and the church was very much the center of their lives." Following a Christian wedding ceremony, Antone and Rima returned to Canada to resume his work there.

"After fourteen and a half years of medical training, finally it was time to go home, and home meant Jordan, for East Jerusalem was then part of Jordan. The Minister of Health had never heard of neurosurgery; there were no neurosurgeons anywhere in Jordan. It took me six months to convince him we needed to have a neurosurgeon in that country of nearly three million people, and for the next thirteen years I was the only neurosurgeon in the entire country. After working for a while in the government hospital I moved to Augustana Lutheran Hospital, run by the German Lutheran Church, on the Mount of Olives. This hospital was well equipped, but by 1961 it was overrun with the needs of thousands of refugees. I volunteered to do all the surgery needed for the refugees for fifty dollars a month. I would find support for my wife and three sons from a few private patients who were nonrefugees.

"The last twenty years of my life have been the most dramatic and challenging period, living and working on the West Bank under military occupation, trying to accomplish what at times seems an impossible task—to perform about seventy-five major brain operations a year along with endless other neurosurgical operations. I feel utter despair at times, for all that I can accomplish in a year or in ten years is wiped out, in terms of numbers, when one destructive air raid takes place and so many lives are lost or wounded. I get angry over the futility of war, as I think all Christians should. Ten years ago, at the very height of my career, something of dramatic importance happened to me and to my brother who was a general surgeon in the Baptist Hospital in Gaza.

"I received a phone call one morning that a hand grenade had been thrown into the hospital grounds and in a flash of time my surgeon brother had lost his right leg and his right hand. I found it necessary to take him to Denmark to have two prosthetic appliances fitted. His career as a surgeon was over, but because he is a Tarazi, he wouldn't give up. He immediately began to retrain as a dermatologist, which he jokingly said, 'I can do well enough with only one good leg and one good hand.' "

While in Denmark, Antone discovered he had cancer. The shock of the pathology findings was great indeed. "It was decided that I would need to go almost immediately to New York to the world-famous Sloan-Kettering hospital for major surgery. Rima, my partner, accompanied me to New York for the six-and-a-half-hour operation. Here I met for the first time friends connected with the

United Methodist Board of Missions who had for some years been financing some of the work that I was doing in Jerusalem. I was able to return to my work, but I faced the same kind of uncertainty about my future as my brother did. He had returned already to his hospital in the Gaza.

"Some years later the malignancy had spread again, and further surgery was necessary on one of my lungs, followed by deep X-ray therapy and chemotherapy. Over the last ten years, these bouts with cancer have interrupted my practice, but I feel God has spared me for a definite purpose. I have to go on at least until some other young neurosurgeons can take my place.

"My family rallied around me. They loved me. They wanted me to go on with my task. My wife Rima, who has a very strong fighting spirit, said, 'We have to go on as long as we can, because our people need us.' " Ten years after his initial traumatic bout with cancer, Antone Tarazi is on the job, in deep serenity that confounds at times both his family and the many friends who surround him with their love.

I asked Antone what the most important things are to him in his life. He said, "First of all, of course, my faith. I know God is with me. God gave me two skilled hands. I have to use them for the purpose of healing. My wife Rima, whose music is an endless inspiration to me. I have to talk about my four boys. We are very blessed by our sons. They have their father's stamina and their mother's serenity and determination. Three of them have graduated from my alma mater, McGill. One of them today works in Saudi Arabia in the oil fields. The second is an architect in Florida. The third will soon complete his engineering studies. The fourth is getting ready to go to McGill next year.

"Everyone is aware of the hardships we Palestinians are

experiencing on the West Bank and Gaza. This brings me back again to the relationship of life and neurosurgery. To me, as a surgeon, the destruction of human life and the wasting of our natural resources degrades human values. As a medical person, I refuse to accept this.

"It's very hard for me today to accept the situation the way it is. Suffering and uncertainties confront all of us Palestinians. We simply want to be ourselves. We want to decide our own future. I refuse to despair. This is our homeland; we've been here, it seems to me, forever. The church must stand with the poor and the powerless. This time seems for some of us a period rather like that of our Lord in the Garden of Gethsemane."

It was time to leave the hospital, but Antone wanted to show me one or two more things before we said good-bye. We left the hospital on the Mount of Olives and drove through the crowded streets of the city and then turned north along the West Bank until we came to Ramullah where the Tarazis live. Antone and his wife have done most of the work in building their lovely home. He wanted to show me one of the secrets of his quietness and peaceful spirit. As we opened the gate and walked into the entrance, I could see at a glance what he really meant, for here was a magnificent rose garden, perhaps one of the most beautiful in the whole area. He had personally planted every one of these roses, and he had tended them very carefully. After long hours in the operating theater fighting for his patient's life, this was where he could come, find quiet, and work with his beloved plants.

Following a delightful dinner, we sat in the garden. Just inside the door Rima sat at her piano. She played, singing one of her own compositions written in the minor key that is so characteristic of Middle Eastern music. She sang of days of loneliness, agony, and pain, describing the feelings of countless numbers of the Palestinian people. Antone softly translated the Arabic for me in the quietness of that evening hour. Then she sang too of hope, and how much greater is "he that is with us than he that is in the world." It was on this note of quiet assuredness and hope and dignity that the music drew to an end. Suddenly the phone rang; the hospital was calling. One of the patients had taken a turn for the worse. Antone left to go back to Makassed, once again at the bedside of a fellow Palestinian. He would spend the rest of the night there, using all the miracles of modern medicine, armed with a deep confidence and hope that life would go on. The spiritual secret of Antone and Rima Tarazi is that they feel they have been given great talents, not for privilege and for personal aggrandizement, but for responsibility to stay with their people and to struggle to give them the dignity that is rightfully theirs.

We shook hands and said good-bye. It seemed very normal that we should also pause for a moment and bow our heads and ask God as the psalmist did so long ago to guide us through the valley of the shadow of death and to fear no evil and to know the same God would watch over this family as he does over all of us who put our trust in him.

Toshihiro "Tom" Takami

"God found me and caught me."

You did not choose me; I chose you, and appointed you to go and bear much fruit, the kind of fruit that endures. And so the Father will give you whatever you ask of him in my name.

—John 15:16 (TEV)

This chapter could well be entitled, "From Zen Buddhist Priest to Director of a Third World Rural Training Center." That would tell a great deal, for the life of Toshihiro Takami is an amazing story of a man whose testimony is, "I became convinced that I could never find God, grasp God by my own strength. It was God who found and caught me to use for the best purpose. Why I became a Christian is very plain. It is because God exists, and God found and caught me. God sought me."

Eighty-five miles north of Tokyo is the county seat of Nishinasuno. It is a busy, prosperous town serving a most important agricultural region. On the outskirts of the town is a large signboard that reads, "Asian Rural Institute." Driving into the compound, one moves into a fascinating world—a unique center in Japan, perhaps the most unusual anywhere in the Third World. Here you will meet young men and women from seventeen or eighteen different countries not only across the Asian continent but from as far away as West Africa. They have come here recruited by their churches to study new methods of food production, organizing cooperatives, handcrafts—a great variety of skills, which they then take back to their own countries as part of God's answer to the never-ending struggle to improve the quality of life for the people whom they serve. This amazing center, which for twenty-five years has trained hundreds of young men and women, principally in Asia but now in Africa also, is really the heartbeat of one unique Japanese Christian.

I have known Toshihiro Takami for exactly twenty years. I well remember the first time that I met this rather short man with strong, rugged features. We bowed deeply, as Asians always do, greeted one another, and talked about how one could build islands of hope in a sea of despair. "Tom" Takami, an extraordinary missionary, wanted to have a center where the rich agricultural experience of the Japanese people, which makes them able to literally produce more food per acre than any other nation in the world, could be shared. He felt this expertise in all its facets should be shared with the rest of the developing world.

Soon after we met, I learned of his concern over not having a home for his bride-to-be. The funds were found from friends in Europe and concerned churches everywhere. Whenever we see each other, we laugh about the fact that when he and his lovely wife built their new home, I was invited as their first guest to use their O *Furo*, the traditional Japanese hot tub. In the twenty years that have elapsed, the Asian Rural Institute has become a key center to which young men and women come, learn, and return to their homes with new inspiration and new hope. If there were ever two hands used for God in an amazing way, they are the hands of this man.

I felt that his own story is so unusual that I asked him to tell it. As he recounts the amazing things that have happened in his life, one can only give thanks to the God who continues to inspire and to use him.

"I was born in Manchuria, not in Japan. My parents were Japanese, so I am also Japanese. I grew up in Manchuria (Northeast China), living there for about ten years. We came to Japan because my father went broke in his business; as long as I can remember, my family has been poor, and to the present has never been rich in material wealth. When we came back here we were really penniless. I remember my mother taking our clothes to the pawn shop after dark to get some money to buy some food for the next day. When I finished grade school in the small town of Maizuru, north of Kyoto on the Japan Sea (a former naval base), I had no hope of going to high school, and of course my parents never thought they could send me. But I was lucky to be chosen as a scholarship student to receive help, to receive a free education in the city of Kyoto. One very important condition was attached to the offer: I was required to leave my home, sever my relationship with my family, enter a Zen monastery, and live as a student monk. From there they would help me to go to school to receive public high school education. Because education meant so much to us all, we accepted those terms. I think even today in Japan that education is a great privilege, but to us it was a *real* privilege.

"Later, a few years ago, when I lived in a small village in Bangladesh (then East Pakistan) I found many village people trying to send only one person to high school and then on to college. The whole family and relatives, maybe thirty or fifty people, would sacrifice. For example, the rest of the children would not go to school beyond third grade so they could just send one person, the oldest boy, to high school and college. I felt much at home living in that kind of situation.

"It was a sad occasion and very difficult for me to leave my mother, father, sister, and brothers, but because of this education, I left my family and went to Kyoto. I spent the following five years in the Zen monastery and lived as a student monk. From the monastery I went on to one of the very good high schools in Kyoto, so I received a very good education and at the same time experienced Zen monastic life. I spent many hours in meditation, sitting still for hours every day. I also learned how to live the life of Zen. It's just sitting still. It was a strict discipline in life. I was supposed to practice Zen even in action. I learned patience. I also learned how to appreciate the beauty of nature and how to be a part of this natural life. It took effort to do that. It does not come naturally to us, and I think I learned that. For instance, every day we cleaned the landscape garden. It's supposed to symbolize the beauty of nature, but you just don't let nature take care of it; that is, when the leaves fall on the ground, you sweep. In autumn the leaves start falling every day. You sweep every corner, every bit, even between the branches of those very fine-branched azaleas. You pick up all those leaves, every one of them, out of every corner, every space. Then, after taking all those leaves off the ground, this landscape garden in autumn without any leaves does not look natural. So we would go around shaking new leaves on to the ground. There is symbolic meaning. The beauty of nature, I think, is the combination of things of nature and our efforts to appreciate it.

"In the spring we would squat on the ground for hours after school under the sun in the beautiful moss-covered garden. The green looked like a carpet. In the spring the weeds start growing, and if you let the weeds grow taller than the moss, they will destroy it. So when the weed buds are about the same size and color as the moss, you have to identify every one of those, thousands of those. Pressing down the moss with one hand to protect it, you then pick the weeds one by one with a thin bamboo spatula. *That* taught me patience! I learned a great deal about moss, the winds, the birds, sounds, and all that. Even today I long to spend at least some time in the garden working with the soil, working with the flowers and things.

"I think that monastic discipline is very important for us today, especially for us Protestants. We seem to be losing discipline in our lives, losing the ability to sit really still and look at something or nowhere; we need that kind of discipline that will keep us free, a free individual under God. I think it takes much discipline to do it. We also need discipline to avoid being captured and moved by certain rules and logic that we invent and impose upon ourselves. Sometimes we try to excuse our own actions because we are not free or disciplined enough to be true human beings. I think I learned some of those things from my Zen experience.

"That experience lasted only about five years. Then it was getting towards the end of World War II. Japan was fighting and tremendous pressure was put on us, especially young boys, to go into the armed services. I'm not a very brave man in that way, so I tried to stay away from the armed services for as long as possible. But finally the draft paper came, and I thought that rather than being drafted I should enlist. So, after receiving the draft paper, I voluntarily enlisted. Since I had already graduated from high school and my mathematical ability was not too bad, I was qualified to become a special student to study radar. Radar then was a very new means of warfare, especially for Japan, and was a very important subject to learn. So I was ordered to stay in school until the end of the war and study electronics and radar operation. I was only about nineteen years old. Many of my friends who were drafted and sent to the front didn't come back. I was saved.

"I was living in Yokohama. From the Japan seaside, north of Kyoto, I came to Fujisawa. I think that today it is the United States Naval Communications Center, formerly the site of the Japanese Naval Radar Center. The war ended while I was there, and I went back to my family in Maizuru. Upon returning to my family, I found that we had lost our father during the war. Later, a younger brother died from sickness and malnutrition, a really tragic situation. We had not been able to get them food. We were eating weesa and just a bit of rice and things. My younger brother contracted appendicitis, and because we could give him no medical care, he suffered a slow death for about one year. Finally, his whole body was affected with several holes producing pus, and after the war, he died. If we had known that penicillin was available through the occupation forces, maybe something could have been done. The United States Army people came to our place to headquarter there, but we were very much afraid because we were told that they would kill everyone. So we just stayed inside the house and remained quiet. My younger brother died from sickness and also from fear. I remained quiet. I found myself, despite all the Zen discipline, becoming a very wicked person.

"When we were hungry I often went to the faraway mountains to pick young leaves and young grass for eating. We were very hungry, and I was quite selfish. I only wanted to get food for myself, not for my family or even for my brother who was suffering tremendously. When I think of how wicked I could be in a hungry situation, I realize even today that I cannot be a good and righteous man without help from God and my fellow persons.

"Few jobs were available in those days, so I did all sorts of jobs: black marketing, carrying fish, potatoes, or rice from the village to the cities to sell. In exchange we would get something else. I did some coal carrying, but mostly I worked as offshore labor. It was a hard job, but at least I could get money and food; hard laborers received extra rations from the government ration office. This hard labor made my body extremely strong. When I was in high school during the war, I wasn't very good in physical exercises and I made the lowest marks. I was the slowest runner in the whole class, and I couldn't do even one chin-up. Experiencing the war and hard offshore labor made my body tough. If I didn't do my share, I'd be kicked out; the competition was very strong among those day laborers.

"After this, I began depending on this physical strength. Sometimes I couldn't find any job. Luckily, because we were living near the sea, I could cross two mountains to the seashore every day on foot, then dive for clams. No one taught me how to swim; necessity taught me. I knew the clams were there, because I saw men swimming and diving for them. I thought that was a good thing to do, so I learned how. I sometimes carried two big sacks of clams on my shoulders over the two mountains back to my town and sold them in exchange for salt or rice. I did this kind of thing to support my family. Often, I was in danger of being drowned, because the wind or tide changed suddenly, or a sudden change in water temperature made my body stiff, making it hard to swim back to shore. This was before I became a Christian, but it seems to me that in this situation I learned how to look earnestly for help and how to pray. I didn't know whom to call, but when I was in the ocean water I was desperately looking for help. I always found some extra strength to swim back or walk along the bottom of the sea to the shore. This whole experience taught me something very precious.

"During those years I worked at many different jobs. Sometimes it meant telling lies in order to find work so my family could eat. One day I found out from the classified ads of the Mainichi English newspaper that a missionary at Kobe College was looking for a cook. I thought that this would be the right kind of job, and I would try it. Opportunities come to us unexpectedly, and we have the freedom to seize them by stepping forward. So I had an interview with Mr. Albert Farout, and that is a time when I told a lie, that I was a cook. He believed me. I had had some experience cooking in the Zen temple. The monks took turns cooking, but mostly they just watched the rice cook. I learned some English in high school before the war, so I could handle some conversation, and I said that I could cook. He was desperate. He was a single man, and even today I think he doesn't know how to make coffee. He said, 'Okay, come back tomorrow, and you will start.' So on the way from this Kobe College, I went to a big book store in Osaka, right in front of the Central Station, and I bought *The Fanny Farmer Cookbook.* Then I used a dictionary and translated the recipes into Japanese every night, and for some time I never served the same kind of breakfast or lunch. I think that to this day he believes that I'm a professional cook.

"When I began working for this man, my life began to change. I saw that he trusted me. When I said I was a cook, he said, 'Okay'; he fixed a salary and hired me. When I went with all my dirty clothes and one pair of torn rubber boots to wear, he said, 'Okay, you will start living with me in the same house.' That house is still there in Kobe College. Next to his room he fixed my room. This was the first time in my life that I had a private room. He bought a new desk, chairs, curtains, bedding, everything. Then he gave me a large amount of money and a small notebook to keep accounts. He said my responsibility was to keep the house, plan meals, write menus, do the shopping, keep all records in the book, pay the bills, and report only once a month to him.

"I never met this kind of person before. I was ready to cheat and I knew how. But when I experienced such trust, this really began to change my own life. I couldn't cheat this person. I began to trust this person, and I also began to trust myself.

"A very interesting thing was that he never told me to come to church with him. But I saw him reading the Bible in English, and I saw him going to church every Sunday, although at first I didn't know where he was going. I asked him to take me to the church someday—the Japanese church. The sermon preached by Dr. Hatanaka, president of Kobe College, was impressive, so I kept going. I began going to an English Bible study at the same church (Kyoto Kyokai), conducted by a lady missionary from Kobe College.

"I didn't have much time to buy a copy of the Bible in Japanese; also, I was so used to leading a very poor life that I thought the Bible was something I really shouldn't spend money on. So I got a free copy of the Bible from a missionary, a small, pocket-sized New Testament, published by the Massachusetts Bible Society, headquartered in Boston. Later, I wrote a letter of appreciation to them after I had become a Christian. It was a small Bible, and I began reading that Bible with the help of the dictionary. When I came to the Gospel of John, this particular book spoke to me directly, and many times I had a very strong spiritual experience. Often, when I was reading a passage, I felt like I was being exposed—that God in Christ was speaking to me directly. When I felt that I was being exposed, I felt I could hide nothing; everything about myself was known to somebody else—God—and I was filled with fear, a special kind of fear. I'm sure you have also experienced it. It's not an ordinary kind of fear; everything about yourself is known by God and you cannot hide. It's very dreadful.

"And so, today I can truly confess with the psalmist that every hair of mine is numbered by God. I can sing and praise and pray with the psalmist:

> O Lord, thou hast searched me and known me!
> Thou knowest when I sit down and when I rise up;. . .
> For thou didst form my inward parts,
> thou didst knit me together in my mother's womb.
> I praise thee, for thou art fearful and wonderful.
> Wonderful are thy works!
> Thou knowest me right well;
> my frame was not hidden from thee,
> when I was being made in secret,
> intricately wrought in the depths of the earth. . . .
> How precious to me are thy thoughts, O God! . . .
> Search me, O God, and know my heart!
> Try me and know my thoughts!
> And see if there be any wicked way in me,
> and lead me in the way everlasting!
>
> —Psalm 139:1–2, 13–15, 17, 23–24

I join the psalmist; I join crowds of the saints of the past, present, and future in this prayer. These are now my prayers.

"Often when I was reading the Bible, I had to close it because it was so powerful that I could not keep reading, but this same experience urged me to read on. I learned a great deal from the Bible. Also, this book, especially Paul's experience, spoke to me in relation to the experiences I had had before coming to Kobe College; all the life that I had thus far experienced became meaningful. Finally I asked the pastor of the church to let me join and receive baptism. We had a very interesting argument. I was formerly a Zen monk. I said that the Bible tells us that if we are baptized by the Spirit, we are already a Christian. 'Why do we have to go through this ritual in the church?' I asked. 'Well,' Dr. Hatanaka said, 'if you feel like it, that's all right; you have been baptized by the Spirit. That may be true. But how can I tell that you have been baptized already unless you are ready to confess before the public in this ceremony?'

"He said it was like a marriage ceremony. Two persons may say that they love each other, so they just get married and don't have a ceremony. But how do they know they love one another unless they are ready to stand before God and before the public to go through this ceremony and make a declaration to the people? I thought this was very good advice. The next Sunday I received baptism in the church and became a professing Christian.

"Later, because of Mr. Farout's efforts, I was introduced to the Nebraska Congregational Church Youth Group, the Pilgrim Fellowship. They became interested in helping me to get a college education. They had a work day for Christ, but later they changed it to a work day for 'Tommy,' and they raised money to pay my way to the United States. I entered Doane College, a small Congregational college in Crete, Nebraska. I went to college for four years there.

"After that I came back to Japan to spend one year. At that time I worked as one of the editorial staff members of the English Mainichi newspaper in Osaka. Then I felt a calling for the ministry. I went back to the United States and received theological education at the Yale Divinity School.

"My decision to become a full-time Christian worker or minister and to continue in it is not just my own decision. It is God calling for sure, but to me it is also a decision of the group, of all those people who helped me at various times to receive an education, of all those friends in Nebraska, in Connecticut, in many lands, and surely my wife and children. All these people have had a meaningful part in my making the decision. I think it is one of those decisions that the people of God make to let one person stand up for the Christian ministry.

"So when I go anywhere, whether it is Bangladesh or Thailand or the Philippines, I feel that I am really going with the people of God, the church. I can think of myself today only in that category. I'm not working alone; I am part of this great work being done by the church. Every time I have to make a decision, it is really a group decision, the people of God deciding together; I have one small, but important, part in this kind of decision making.

"I realize that I carry many of the past experiences in the form of scars, because I worked as a day laborer in black marketing, cheating this person and that person, and also being betrayed or cheated by others. Every bit of these experiences left me many scars.

"I am reminded very much of the story of Jacob wrestling with the angel. After this mighty struggle he is disjointed, and he limps along, but he goes across the river with his own people. I'm sure the rest of his life he limped along. I think I am very happy to limp along with the rest of the people to cross the river together, to go forward marching toward the kingdom of God.

"When I look back on my past life and my involvement today in so many varied works of the church, I think I really am having a meaningful, joyful, wonderful life. Right now I am going through a difficult life together with the students and faculty in a school which has all kinds of problems. Sometimes I am tempted to seek an easier way of living the life of faith, but when I think of my calling as a minister of the church, I know my calling is to make all these things meaningful, all these experiences Christian. I firmly believe that through my own life and the lives of so many others, everything in Christ is 'yes'; nothing is wasted. So we just keep struggling."

The story of "Tom" Takami's life still goes on in a marvelous way. Just a few days ago when I was in West Africa, I met with six of the alumni of the Asian Rural Institute working in Liberia in the rural areas and as soon as I mentioned Tom Takami's name their faces lit up. One of them said, "This man is truly inspired by God in what he is doing in far-off Japan."

"Tom" Takami has a dream that the Asian Rural Institute, unique as it is, can be duplicated in other parts of the world. Before he retires, which is some years away, he hopes that similar centers for young men and women can be established in Africa, Latin America, and the Middle East. All would be part of a Christian network of rural centers that bring together men and women from surrounding nations to discuss their problems, to work together in the fields, and to go back to their own homes with new determination to close the gap between the world of the haves and the world of the have-nots.

Esther Park

A Foundation under Her Dreams

But they who wait for the Lord
shall renew their strength,
  they shall mount up with wings like eagles,
they shall run and not be weary,
  they shall walk and not faint.
—Isaiah 40:31

Eighty years ago a Methodist pastor, his wife, and five children came ashore in Honolulu as immigrants from Korea. They were immigrants with a mission, because they were sent by their church to minister to the large number of Korean laborers attracted by the offer of jobs in the growing sugar cane industry. This family's entire life would be devoted to the task of building Christ's kingdom in the hearts of the Hawaiian Korean people.

The Reverend Mr. Park carried in his arms from the ship their youngest, year-old daughter Esther. Little did they dream that following two world wars and almost on the eve of the Korean War, Esther would return to Korea to be a symbol of hope and self-giving love to hundreds of thousands of Korean women and girls. If there were ever two tireless, dedicated hands for God's service, they belong to Esther Park.

From her family Esther acquired the spirit of self-giving love and a deep personal commitment to Jesus Christ. Her life was to be almost equally divided between Hawaii and South Korea. Following graduation from the University of Hawaii, she joined the staff of the Honolulu YWCA. In the years that followed, her experiences in that multi-racial society prepared her for her major task in Korea of training young women to take their places as leaders in what had traditionally been a male-dominated society. Even today, the Korean church, now the fastest-growing church in Asia, has great difficulty in accepting women as equals in leadership roles.

The amazing life of this American-Korean woman has been well documented in a book titled *Life Abundant*, but unfortunately, it is published only in Korean and somehow fails to capture the inner spirit of Esther Park. This skilled builder, the dreamer of a new role for Korean women and girls as co-equals in the building of the nation, saw the need to put a foundation under her dreams.

My friendship with Esther goes back twenty years when I first met her in Seoul. Over a very simple meal she said, "You are from the World Council of Churches, and it is committed to strengthening the work of the church universal. We need your help right now. There are great Christian institutions in Korea. We have the largest women's university in the world, Ewha, with 16,000 students; and other great centers of Christian higher education. Our church is one of the fastest growing in Asia—many, many wonderful things are happening here despite the long tragic years of the Japanese occupation and the devastation of the Korean War. Yet our hearts are heavy with grief. We are only thirty-five miles from the demilitarized zone and the North Korean frontier. I don't know whether in my lifetime there will be a unified Korea, even though we want this so desperately to happen. Sixty thousand foreign troops are here under the United Nations' command, and there are 50,000 Korean prostitutes. Our poverty and war weariness is no excuse. I refuse to accept this intolerable situation. We need help to reclaim our young women, to restore them to the abundant life God intended them to have. I want a harvest of hope for our people, not the harvest of shame."

A few months ago, I saw Esther first in her retirement home in Honolulu and, unexpectedly, shortly afterwards in Seoul where at eighty years of age, as vigorous as ever, she was consulting with her Korean colleagues about exciting new plans for Korean women. Reclaiming young women off the streets of Korea's cities was only one of endless ways hope had come to women, young and old, but when I reminded her of our conversation long ago she replied, "Well, 16,000 women have passed through our Kwangju Rehabilitation and Vocational Center, thanks to the help of so many friends. Now our international Women's Center is planning. . ." and off she went with a new enthusiastic plan.

The purpose of this devotional book is not just to write five biographies as such, but to look for a "oneness of the spirit" and to be inspired by their spirituality. What is the inner strength of Esther Park? There is a Korean saying, "Our women may be as beautiful as chrysanthemums, but they have an inner core of steel." I found some of the answers to an understanding of Esther Park in a monthly letter she wrote for many years under the title "Thoughts of the Times." She still occasionally sends out "Thoughts of the Times" to 500 women, for as she laughingly said, "You know God hasn't finished with me yet."

It was a bitterly cold winter day in 1947 when Esther returned to the place of her birth after a forty-five-year absence. The YWCA school was occupied by destitute refugees, as were thousands of other buildings. All she and two Korean women colleagues had for headquarters was a small room with a wood stove to keep them from freezing. Where to begin? What to do? There was a shortage of everything: fuel, light, water, food, clothing, and money. "So we began with a free school for underprivileged children, organizing milk distribution, prayer groups, and church services. Much of what we did was not traditional work, but we were to discover we could not be very traditional if something was to happen.

"Change in people may start very simply: a grandmother learns to read and write for the first time and finds a whole new world opening up before her; a lonely woman finds acceptance in a women's fellowship; a girl in a rural area sent by her family to the city to earn money as a prostitute finds refuge in a YWCA center for the recovery of human dignity and is given vocational training.

"Did pressures and new trends ask of us the utmost in effort, wisdom, and faith? We are aware of the importance of the woman's role in nation building and must reach to help individuals at their level of need. We discovered our task was not to have a nice, well-financed institution with attractive buildings as our fixed goal. Instead, we found we needed to go out to meet the needs of a homeless child, an illiterate mother in a rural village, or a widow in a large city. Reaching out to students struggling to get an education, to working wives and mothers with child care and nutrition, all were our goals. Self-help projects are needed in the struggle against poverty, deprivation, and discrimination.

"Over the next twenty years, promising young graduates from Ewha Woman's University—eighty-six in all—were sent overseas to a number of countries for training in YWCA leadership, for we had a big task to do. In the early postwar years many churches were somewhat aloof, and pastors were suspicious that we were 'social workers,' not an arm of the body of Christ. Yes, urgent social issues needed to be dealt with in Korea regarding women's status and their rights: educating women for their new roles in a rapidly changing political, economic, and social scene; relief work among needy people; milk stations for underprivileged children; care of orphans; work with war widows. Many of the projects begun thirty-five years ago are still being continued, now reaching over 300,000 individuals annually.

"Today we are called to responsibilities such as no previous generation has faced. Anyone who hopes to avoid all failure and misfortune is trying to live in a fairyland. We must not set up for ourselves the impossible ideal of always being successful in everything. Although we cannot always control what happens, we can always control how we respond to our failures; to brood over our failures or mistakes, to reproach ourselves to the point of self-destruction will not get us anywhere. We must develop a bounce, rebounding from defeat as a rubber ball rebounds. We must learn the lessons of failure, to build for the future. If we can keep faith in God and in ourselves, nothing can permanently defeat us.

"We experience many suicides among our Korean young people who fail in their exams, because they feel they have let down their families who sacrificed everything for their education. I don't know whether this is an oriental philosophy or not, but there seems to be a feeling of absolute helplessness when failure comes. Here is a great testing place for the Christian faith. What does it do with failure?

"When the war in Korea began in 1952, women had no political or economic freedom; they were bound by old traditions and customs. Prayer was their only weapon, as they had little money or other means. All they had was their faith and a burning desire to serve.

"The Korean churches were busy with many things, but the task of bringing abundant life to all women in all circumstances involved a resolute group of Christian women who brought hope and love in the midst of despair, new life, and freedom in the midst of domination and occupation by alien forces.

"Not long ago, a young mother told me that her little four-year-old boy demanded payment for every little thing he was asked to do around the house. It all started when the mother had paid him money to get him to go to the doctor, so for each subsequent visit to the doctor she had to pay him. Later, when he was asked to pick something up off the floor, he asked, 'What is it worth to you?'

"The demand to know 'What is in it for me?' is not just a Korean characteristic. Often, we are all guilty of taking from life, from family, from friends, from the country—with little thought of giving. Millions of people here in Korea are starving, not for bread but for kindness. Bruised spirits long for love. When we choose the way of giving love, we have put ourselves in touch with a supply of love which cannot be exhausted. It does not stop with those who speak the same language. Those who have found the way of giving life and hope and love have the joy of seeing order grow out of chaos—in family life, in international questions. Are we giving persons, or are we taking persons? Try giving away what you have—possessions are the least of it. It is when you give of yourself that you truly give.

"Organizations, like people, tend to go through a cycle of life: a period of vigorous youth; a period of consolidating and strengthening of position; one of conservative forward movement; and finally, a period of living on the gains of productive years. But unlike people whose term of life is limited, organizations often live on for many years after all creative spark has disappeared.

"As we review our years of service to women and girls, we cannot help but ask ourselves, 'What makes the continuance of our mission urgent?' It's possible to be part of the church without much awareness of possible commitment. We must try to produce a real fellowship in the spirit of Jesus. Our direction establishes our uniqueness.

"Recently a Canadian visitor to Korea said to me, 'People in Korea seem very busy. Everyone seems in a hurry.' Many Koreans believe there is no such thing as leisure in this country. Everyone is busy. (Fortunately, it is the women who are involved in the business of everyday living.) Yet, strangely enough, we generally find that the busiest person is the one who comes to help us. She is a growing person living a full life.

"I believe we are born wanting to belong. It is against our nature to be alone, though some individuals would have us think they can live by themselves, isolated from the rest of the world. In spite of the boasts of self-sufficiency and strength, in the final analysis we can't live alone. So many of us are at war with ourselves and our neighbors. The mental ills, nervous tensions, conflicts, and anxieties which beset persons and make them insecure are the result of this longing to achieve security, to feel they belong. Unless persons feel that they belong somewhere, unless life has meaning, they are in danger of being overcome by feelings of insignificance.

"I have always believed in dreams. I dream dreams about the YWCA and its work in Korea. I have faith in God who will grant me grace sufficient for my needs. And I believe in myself, that with work well planned and worked at diligently, my dreams will come true. This has been true throughout my life, and this is what I wish for Korea—that it too will have dreams of a world of peace and justice, not only for Korea but for the world. They must have faith in God, but faith without works is dead."

To Christian women, the program of education was a symbol of freedom. The application of Christian values to everyday life led them into working on child welfare laws, establishment of a family court system where previous laws discriminated against women in matters of inheritance, headship of the family, and ownership of property. In the '80s the National Association of the YWCA works with 600,000 members, a far cry from 1947 when three women crowded around a wood stove and dreamed of a new Korea.

"The sign of peace is love. It cannot be controlled by computers. It depends ultimately on the human heart, on the love of people for people, on their acceptance of one another as children of God.

"Today has waited from all eternity to confront us. When I wake up in the morning, I say to myself, 'This is the day God has made for me to enjoy. I am going to make the day really count.' The quality of life is more important than the quantity. One day is all for which I am responsible. This simplifies my task, for what I do today will become a part of my life tomorrow."

This last paragraph is an eloquent testimony from a woman who found the secret of how to put a foundation under her dreams.

Frank Field

"I'm only a catalyst."

He must increase, but I must decrease.
—John 3:30

The interview with Frank Field was slowly drawing to a close as we sat in his apartment in Polegate on the south coast of England. Joining us in the conversation was Frank's pastor who sat there wide-eyed, not realizing what an extraordinary person he had in his congregation each Sunday. Indeed, to meet Frank Field is to be rather disarmed by his directness of speech. Yet, there is a certain shyness in his manner, for Frank Field is certainly not a raconteur, the kind of person who will keep you enthralled by telling you fascinating stories. He could, however, because his life is a very unusual one.

We recounted together where Frank Field has served

 in the last forty years: Burma, India, Japan, Australia, Ethiopia, Fiji Islands, Hong Kong, Bolivia, Bangladesh. He will share amazing stories about every one of these countries. Then, after you've been with him for a while and you are moved by his amazing experiences as the servant of Jesus Christ, you have to ask, "Frank, what makes you tick? How is it you've done all these extraordinary things?" His answer is the same today as when I first met him thirty-one years ago in Malaysia. "I'm only a catalyst," he replies. "I'm like an interpreter. I make things happen, but it's not me at all. I try never to be photographed. I am really nothing special at all; God is all. I've tried throughout these years to allow God to work in me." If you want to praise and or say anything good to Frank Field, he will want you to give praise and thanks to Frank's Lord and Master.

That is a good point of connection with the text under his name. It was John the Baptist who, recognizing the Lord of Life, cried out, "He must increase, but I must decrease" (John 3:30). Frank Field's two hands have touched the lives of countless numbers of people, and from time to time I meet some of these people.

To a fishing village in the New Territory near Hong Kong called St. Andrew's-by-the-Sea Frank went on behalf of The United Methodist Committee on Relief. There, he directed the building of that village for 800 destitute fishermen and their families whose boats had rotted out. For the first time in their lives they were forced to give up fishing and live on the land in permanent homes. When you mention Frank Field, their eyes light up and they say, "Yes, we remember him." Walk through the village of Barrackpore, eighty miles north of Calcutta where 10,000 people live who were taken out of the worst slums in that great city of ten million people and started to live again. When you mention Frank

Field, and it's been almost twenty years since Frank was there, they remember him; and this in itself is quite remarkable.

Frank Field was born into a very poor home in 1911. He remembers his father going off to the battlefields in France, and just two days before World War I ended, his father was killed in the mud and debris of France. At the age of seven, Frank became responsible for his younger brothers and sisters; as he likes to say, "I grew up overnight so that I could become the head of the family." Because his father had been a mail carrier in the town of Eastbourne, the town set up a memorial fund for mail carriers killed in the war. Frank received one of those scholarships and went off to secondary school. Without that scholarship, he almost certainly would never have made it. Through the influence of Christian teachers and the family atmosphere of the school, Frank made his commitment to Jesus Christ and on graduating went to work in the slums of the east end of London helping to run a boys club. He worked as a social worker and advocate for the boys when they were in trouble with the police authorities, and also as an organizer of scouting groups. This would be Frank's life for the next twenty years, until World War II began. Then, like all able-bodied men, he was called for military service. He was sent with the Thirty-third Army Corps under General William Slim to Burma. His responsibility was as a lay missionary, social worker, and counselor with the men in an extraordinary organization called Toc H. This was a British Christian service agency born in the trenches of World War I in Europe and continued throughout the years that followed. With the fall of Mandalay to the Japanese Imperial Forces, the British army was compelled to retreat to India. There Frank spent the remainder of the war. Without having an opportunity to return to England, he left India with an advance group of soldiers to serve with the occupation army in Japan.

All of this: air raid warden in England, boy scout leader, worker in the east end of London slums and with the troops in Burma, India, and Japan, was but prelude for the amazing life that was actually just beginning for this young Englishman. For a short time he took up farming in the south of England until he was challenged by a person returning from Malaysia who had come into his community. By 1950, Malaysia was in turmoil as the struggle went on with communist forces, almost entirely made up of Chinese, who sought to overthrow the British rule in Malaysia and Singapore. Inspired by the liberation of the People's Republic of China in 1949, they hoped to bring that rich area of the world, which provides 40 percent of the world's natural rubber supply, into the communist orbit. It was soon clear to the commanding officer of the British in Malaysia in 1950, General Sir Gerald Templar, that if the internal struggle was going to come to an end, the key was to win the hearts and minds of the people. Not all the military forces at the disposal of England could bring peace in a land where ambushes, train derailments, arson, and murder were daily occurrences in what was known for the next several years as "The Emergency."

As the authorities saw it, the key to stabilizing the country was to move 500,000 rural Chinese living on the edge of the jungle in Malaysia into protected villages. Behind barbed wire, floodlit at night and patrolled twenty-four hours of the day by heavily armed troops, the Chinese could carry out a certain amount of farming but would be removed from the direct influence of the communist insurgency groups. Frank was recruited as a resettlement officer. His assignment was to go to Ipoh, the capital of the state of Perak, where for the next four years he was to live with the people in resettlement camps, helping them to adjust to the new life. His projects included helping to establish schools for their children, clinics and pure water supplies for the community, and giving them the ability to continue outside the barbed wire fence in the daytime to produce food not only for themselves but for the surrounding towns as well.

Frank was qualified for this job: he knew how to organize people, and having organized them, he knew how to persuade them that it was really their idea all along. They had thought of the plan, they were going to take full credit for it, and there would be no demurring on the part of this man. He would just smile to himself and say, "Thank you God for guiding me." Because when you talk with Frank Field, no matter what the conversation is, sooner or later in a perfectly natural way he's going to talk about being guided by the Holy Spirit. He says in a very straightforward way, "All my life I have been guided by the spirit of God. Whenever I have resisted God's guidance I've gotten into deep trouble; when I've accepted that guidance, things have gone very well indeed." With this simple faith and an acceptance of the guiding hand of God in his role as the catalyst, Frank was to spend four amazing years claiming nothing for himself. He ran through a number of ambushes; in one ten-day period he was shot at an average of every two days. The other eleven British resettlement officers working in the state of Perak saw their job essentially as resettling people, helping to put them, with military force if necessary, in communities of 3,000 to 10,000 people per village. Then they could only hope that the resettled groups would be content to stay there and not become the eyes and ears of the terrorists or provide food, money, and recruits for them.

This is where I first met Frank. One Sunday morning

 he drove up and out of his jeep came ten young Chinese with him. To see Frank at the wheel with sometimes ten more people piled into his jeep was something you just accepted. Frank came to church and introduced the young boys of whom he was very proud. They were delighted to get out of the barbed wire protected village for a few hours to come into town. If they didn't understand everything going on in the church service, they certainly understood that after church they would sit and eat ice cream and wonder who this strange Englishman was who really cared about their people and wanted to live in the villages with them rather than in the security of the hostel in the big city where most of the other British lived.

Thirty years after Frank had arrived in Malaysia, he went back there. The day we were having our visit together he had just returned from Kuala Lumpur, the capital of Malaysia. "What did you find, Frank," I asked, "when you went back to Malaysia after an almost thirty-year absence?"

"Well," he said, "I didn't meet many foreigners, as I spent all my time with my Chinese friends, and it was really quite remarkable." Back in 1952 he had devised, completely without any authority, an imposing-looking certificate which gave these landless farmers a title for a thirty-year lease on a patch of land along the edge of the jungle. He went back this time and these people still had the framed titles which the government had honored and extended to ninety years. These formerly landless people who had spent four frightened years in the protected villages were now prosperous farmers, and their children were graduating from schools in the area. Their children had even gone to the university, and it was impossible that they would ever forget Frank Field whose life had been shared with them. After living for four years on the edge of the jungle in central Malaysia, England seemed a very tame place indeed. It proved to be so, for on his return to England he became restless, and I rather suspect a little fed up with the notoriously damp English climate. Before long, Frank was packing his bags, this time striking out for northern Australia.

He had heard that it was possible to get title to land at a very reasonable cost. The marvelous brochures had also assured him and others that if they went to Darwin, the capital of Northern Territory in Australia, they could buy fifty-acre plantations for next to nothing and there begin to produce magnificent pineapples which were all guaranteed, as far as purchase was concerned, by the people who sold you the land. Before long you would have it made—at least, that's what the brochure said. Frank went off to be a pineapple farmer. There has come into our American vocabulary the word *scam*. The pineapple plantation prospectus proved to be a scam operation. Undeterred, Frank turned to working with the forestry department in planting tropical trees to hold back the desert on the outskirts of Darwin.

This proved to be an engrossing task until 1963 when he accepted the invitation to go to Calcutta, India, on behalf of the World Council of Churches. His new job was to help direct a project called "Operation Dayah," an attempt at what everyone thought in Calcutta would be an utterly impossible task: taking 10,000 people out of the worst slums in the city. These were truly the poorest of the poor, huddled in the Sealdah Railway Station where they had come as destitute refugees from East Pakistan, now emerging as the new nation of Bangladesh. The project involved taking them out of this terrifying slum to an area eighty miles away in the country where they could create a new community with new industries. This project would help these people become an island of hope in what was otherwise a sea of despair.

Anyone who ever goes to Calcutta experiences a great trauma in encountering such desperate poverty. It would take a whole book to describe what happened in moving those 10,000 people. The first thing, of course, was to win their confidence. This was a repetition of the same philosophy experienced in Malaysia where it was necessary to win the hearts and minds of the people. A talented Indian woman, the wife of a doctor, agreed to go and live in the slum with the people and to get to know each one of the 2,000 families, and then, nearly a year later, on three consecutive nights between midnight and three in the morning, with specially chartered trains, move the whole 10,000 out. They were taken to Barrackpore where life really began for them in a very wonderful way. It was also done to provoke the municipality of Calcutta into doing something about their own people. They were very difficult people even for Frank Field to handle. He said they had been greatly brutalized by their experience of years of destitution. In a moment of inspiration he took into the area a large poster of the well-known symbol of the boat without sails and cross in the center. The symbol is indelibly identified with the ecumenical movement. But his interpreation was, "We're all in this boat together." In a rather unorthodox interpretation, they were told that the boat had neither sails nor engine. "If we're going to move it, we're going to have to row it out of here ourselves." Somehow they caught the spirit of this man and it all happened.

Twenty years later I went back to Barrackpore and found that the original colony was still there. They were much better off than most of the people in the area through their own hard work. It was interesting to hear a distinguished Indian church leader explain to me how he had conceived the whole plan and seen that it was carried out, how these things really could happen once you had the right idea. I thought, "That's what it's really all about," for this amazing Englishman had persuaded the Indian leaders that it was their idea, that they had it. When I mentioned his name to one or two of the people, their faces lit up. They remembered him, that strange Englishman who worked in an old torn pair of pants, most of the time without a shirt, out there talking to them in a mixture of English, Cantonese, and Burmese and very little of anything else. Yet with this amazing combination of languages, the job had been done, and new life and hope had come to this community.

Frank's next adventure took place in Ethiopia where the assignment was to work with refugees on the border between Ethiopia, the Sudan, and Eritrea. For two years Frank lived in one of the most desolate places in Africa trying to get them to establish some permanent colonies where they could grow food, the children could go to school, and they could change their status from destitute nomads to established village people.

Then came perhaps the single biggest challenge that had come to Frank Field. This was an invitation to go to Hong Kong to help resettle boat people who for generations had spent their lives fishing in the South China Sea but who were now refugees in Hong Kong and mainland China. Inasmuch as St. Andrew is the patron saint of fishermen, it was decided to call the new community St. Andrew's-by-the-Sea. Five villages were established for the refugees, three in Hong Kong and two in Taiwan. All five villages are still in existence today in a slightly different form than they were when first located there. But they are there.

St. Andrew's-by-the-Sea was to prove the most difficult of all to carry out. The problem was to get the five different branches of the Hong Kong government together and get them to agree to make land available, to meet the medical and educational needs of the community, and to help organize the 800 families into a single unit. Fishermen are generally rugged individualists who don't easily work together. Yet, the wonderful day dawned when 800 families came across the estuary in boats, firing off firecrackers, waving brilliantly colored flags, and moved into their new homes. Once again the word came back, "Mission accomplished." "The Holy Spirit is guiding me and I'm ready for the next assignment." So after Calcutta, Ethiopia, and Hong Kong came the most frustrating assignment yet to confront this amazing personality.

The Methodist Missionary Society in London sent an urgent request to UMCOR, New York, to help find a troubleshooter extraordinaire to go to the Fiji Islands.

To the west of Fiji are two very famous islands, Nauru and Ocean Islands. They contained some of the world's richest phosphate deposits which brought a very rich return to the British Phosphate Commission, a joint operation of the New Zealand and Australian governments. When the phosphate had almost all been mined out, 2,000 of the islanders had to be removed to Fiji and then to the island of Rambi to start life again. The problem was that the islanders didn't want to go there. They wanted vast compensation, running into millions of dollars. With the aid of a group of lawyers, they began litigation against the British government which was to go on for several years.

Frank Field's job was very simple. All he had to do was to go to the Fiji Islands and help these people start life anew. However, the islanders wanted to return to their homes, which by this time were almost uninhabitable.

In the two years that followed, Frank's experience working with people over the years made him the ombudsman of the community. It was altogether an incredible experience. The Rambi Island people will never forget this incredible Englishman who was unlike any other government official, and who for days and sometimes weeks was simply with them, sitting where they sat.

Running through all this amazing man's experience as an outstanding troubleshooter and a Christian with an unusual understanding of the gospel is his philosophy of life: "Stop thinking about yourself. Reach out and put your hand in God's hand. Be open to what God wants you to do, and miracles can happen. When you stand with God you are always in the majority, and God is looking all the time for people who will be completely open to his influence, to his Holy Spirit."

"I really am nothing at all," protests Frank when you remind him of the astonishing things that have happened where he has gone. "God is sufficient if you are willing to take no credit for yourself and to stop considering success and just listen. That's all there is to it."

Alain Rocourt

Snatched from the Jaws of Death

The life I now live in the flesh I live by faith in the Son of God.
—Galatians 2:20

Snatched from the jaws of death sounds very dramatic, but it really was for a young Haitian pastor whose remarkable life continues to be a "fragrance unto Christ" in the most desperately poor country in the Western Hemisphere.

In the southern peninsula of Haiti in the town of Jérémie following a political crisis, the community for two months lived under a strict curfew. Fear gripped the entire population. Daily, people were taken from their houses to be executed. All mulattoes (persons of mixed blood) were suspect and their homes put to the torch. Alain Rocourt, a Methodist pastor, was arrested and taken to a common grave already dug, to be summarily shot. At the moment just before death, an official from the local government recognized Alain and shouted out, "It's a mistake, it's the wrong person!" Handcuffed, he was brought before a group of high-ranking army officers and asked if he wanted to say anything. Alain spoke of the church's identification with the powerless and the poor and said that he had no ambition other than that of serving the people in their time of need. Immediately released, he went to his house where his wife and two small children waited. The young pastor knew his life had been spared for a purpose and that never again could he live unto himself. In the words of St. Paul he could say, "The life I now live in the flesh I live by faith in the Son of God" (Gal. 2:20). In the next three months no pastor in the area could function, and Alain and his family remained in a remote mountain village until sanity and peace were restored. What had happened to the church in his absence? The lay preachers had kept the churches going by preaching, teaching, counseling, visiting, comforting. The laity had proved to be "God's frozen assets" which the baptism of suffering had defrosted. This experience would determine the future direction of Pastor Rocourt's life and work. The future growth of the church would need a trained laity, and his task would be to train them. "Why did God rescue me?" This question would haunt him in the years that followed.

Alain tells in very simple, but moving, language his own story.

"When I look back over the past twenty-nine years, I say to myself that I have been a very fortunate man. In a country where the Christian church is the only agency bringing real hope to people in despair, God has given me the privilege of serving him in a ministry that has many forms. In spite of all the problems that I have had to face or the difficulties that may lie ahead, I would not choose to be anywhere else where life might be easier, for God makes all of life very meaningful.

"I was born and grew up in a strong Methodist family. My grandfather, on my mother's side, was in charge for many years of the church in the town of Les Cayes, in the southern peninsula of Haiti. On my father's side, I belonged to a Protestant minority that was known for its evangelical faith and sterling qualities of honesty and loving-kindness. From my father I learned the importance of hard work, the dignity of manual labor at a time when it was despised by middle-class mulatto families. He was very gifted with his hands and very inventive. By profession he was a shoemaker, but he had skills in many other fields, especially agriculture which he loved. From him I inherited that love. He was a sincere friend of the peasants whom he knew well and appreciated at a time when there was a great gulf between the population in town and the rural masses. He faced challenges in life with a will to overcome.

"My mother was a refined and cultured person. She died when I was fifteen, but I remember her very well as a gentle and shy person. She had a heart of gold. I remember vividly how, having found a young and very poor boy lying on the wayside with a festering leg full of small worms, she took him home and looked after him, dressing his wound herself until he was well again. She was the only teacher I ever had for all my primary education.

"The first seven-and-a-half years of my life I spent in the countryside where my parents lived. This gave me a firsthand knowledge of the conditions in which the peasants live and helped me to develop a deep respect for their courage and resilience and kindness. In those early days religion was an important part of my life. For my parents, my older sister, and myself, it was natural to ride on horse or donkey the eight-mile distance from our home to the church in town to attend the Sunday morning service.

"When I was seven years old, my family left the countryside to move to my father's home town, Jérémie, where he opened a small shoe shop. But he kept his interest in agricultural work. In Jérémie the most important factor in my life was, I think, the influence of the Methodist church. The local pastor was a lay preacher, a cousin of my father, a highly cultured man who was a model of Christian gentleness. His moral stature was respected by the population and his gifts as a painter and a pianist were well recognized.

"It was at the Sunday school that I was introduced to the story of Jesus. I also loved to participate in Sunday school competitions and always acted in plays at Christmas fetes. The church in Jérémie was then rather a family affair, a small community eager to preserve its evangelical faith, surrounded as it was by a medieval type of Roman Catholicism. It was puritanical in its outlook and practice and took pride in its cultural superiority. The church had no social outreach. All services were held in French. Those were the days when it would have been unthinkable to conduct a service in the church in the Creole language, which was considered absolutely inferior, although everybody used it.

"Life was hard, materially speaking, but simple and quite happy. However, strict family habits coupled with strong church discipline left their negative marks on my character, making me a shy boy.

"At fourteen I thought it normal to seek membership in the church. After a trial period of three months, but without any special instruction, I was received into membership on Easter Sunday. This only made me more conscious of my duty to maintain the tradition of separation from the world. This too contributed to shaping me into a shy, introverted boy.

"During my year in Port-au-Prince I attended the Methodist church regularly every Sunday; but knowing only a few people in that big church, I always felt out of my depth there. Of course, by correspondence I had kept in close touch with my family and the church at home in Jérémie. I had heard with surprise that, through the witness and preaching of a medical doctor recently appointed to the hospital in Jérémie, quite a new life had come into the congregation. Open-air services were held in some part of the town and quite a few people had professed conversion, people who were from a low social stratum and who were now entering the church. I could hardly imagine what that kind of happening looked like. I had never witnessed a profession of conversion. The only meaning the word then conveyed to me, with my fanatical evangelical frame of mind, was 'leaving the Roman Catholic Church to join the Protestant faithful.' I did not imagine that it had anything to do with a personal encounter with Jesus Christ.

"When I went home for the summer vacation in 1942, the first service I attended was quite an experience. I was amazed to see lots of new faces. Those people were singing Creole hymns lustily and with obvious sincerity, expressing praise to God for their newly found faith. Some of them testified publicly and spontaneously how they had found Christ as their Saviour, and how their lives had been completely changed. I was amazed to discover the existence of a completely new aspect of the religious experience, realizing at the same time that those people possessed something which I lacked: a sense of deliverance and joy, the assurance of Christ present in their lives. I fully realized then that my faith was something of the head, not of the heart, and the challenge came to me, loud and clear. One evening I publicly surrendered my life to the personal Saviour I was meeting for the first time.

"I began to work actively in the evangelistic drive the church was making. My life had taken a significant turn.

"The question, of course, remained. How was I going to earn my living? I would have liked to study medicine, but even if I had managed to pass the stiff entrance examination, my family could not afford to pay for my board and lodging in Port-au-Prince. I had to find a job to earn some money in order to contribute to the family budget and be responsible for even my limited personal needs. But for an inexperienced young man of eighteen, the work market did not seem to offer anything in Jérémie. I did not know what to do, especially since I could not go to Port-au-Prince, where I was sure I could find better opportunities. I grew anxious at times, but I was comforted by the thought that my Lord would show me the direction in which he wanted me to go.

"Unexpectedly, I learned that there was going to be an examination for recruiting an assistant teacher of Latin and French for the secondary school which had been my alma mater in Jérémie. I did not particularly want to be a teacher; in fact, shy as I was and so young, I trembled at the prospect of teaching young people who were almost my age. But there was no other job in sight, so I followed my parents' advice to go and try my luck at that examination. I found it easy enough. I was successful and received notice that I was appointed a teacher in that school. I taught Latin and French there for five years. I enjoyed the atmosphere, the opportunity of enlarging my knowledge. I was also very active in the church as a lay preacher and as a Sunday school teacher. It was such a joy to see the work develop and new outposts created in various areas in the countryside.

"At the same time, I had to think of ways to increase my meager income, but it was obvious that on my teacher's salary I would be unable to create my own family someday. I decided to learn accounting, but I had to do it by correspondence. I took courses from LaSalle Extension University in Chicago. To do that I had to learn English, because the only modern language I had studied in school was Spanish. I studied enough English to be able to follow two courses with LaSalle. I thought then that I was equipping myself in order to be able to have a side job as a part-time accountant in Jérémie. I could never have known that this was one step further God was guiding me in the direction in which he wanted me to go.

"Also during that time, in association with my father and two cousins, I became involved in banana production, thus maintaining the family tradition of deep interest in rural problems and possibilities. This gave me good grounding in situations which, as a minister, I would have to confront.

"Having received my accounting diploma, I sought part-time jobs in Jérémie, but none were available. Also, our hopes of getting good banana crops vanished when a disease destroyed the plantations in the Jérémie area. As a result, hopes of increasing my monthly income were very uncertain. Had this been different, I would probably have wanted to remain in Jérémie all my life. But God had other plans. One Thursday morning when my stepmother arrived from Port-au-Prince, she said to me, 'Alain, there is a good opportunity for you to get a job as Accounting Clerk with the Esso Company in Port-au-Prince. In two days' time the candidates for the post will have to sit for an examination. I think you should have a go at it.' We were at the end of the school year; I could take some days off without any problem. But I hesitated. Was it the proper move to make? I made the matter a subject of prayer. The salary that was being offered was well over twice as much as what I was earning, so the job was very tempting. However, I said to the Lord, 'If this is not your will for me, please let something happen that may make me see it clearly. If I should fail the examination, I would know that you have other plans for me.' I arrived in Port-au-Prince on Saturday morning after a rough sea trip, having been seasick a good deal of the time. I had to go immediately to the Esso headquarters and take the written examination forthwith. It looked simple enough to me, but I wondered if I had much chance competing with several other people from Port-au-Prince. After a few days, the company's manager sent for me and informed me that on the basis of the examination results, the company was giving me the job. I was delightfully surprised.

"With the increase in salary, I had the satisfaction of giving greater financial assistance to my family in Jérémie. The situation there had become economically harder. My father, after my mother's death, had married again and had now four young sons and it was not easy to manage.

"In Port-au-Prince I began to help in the church as a Sunday school teacher and lay preacher. I missed the church in Jérémie, particularly the challenging evangelistic activities. But in Port-au-Prince I met a good number of young persons my age, and I was happy to join the fellowship meetings. My job at Esso was interesting and well paid. I could begin to consider the possibility of creating my own family. Life seemed to be full of happy prospects.

"Convinced that my coming to Port-au-Prince was finally God's doing, I began to wonder whether he had brought me there simply to enable me to earn a better salary. It seemed to me that God must have other reasons as well. One day the thought came to me fairly suddenly: What about giving my whole time to God's work? This meant, of course, offering myself for the ministry. I immediately discarded the idea as being foolish. I was already helping the church by giving as much as possible of my free time; I was also giving generously of my salary to help support the work. Moreover, I had a financial duty towards my family. Last, but not least, I was thinking seriously about marriage. Offering myself as a candidate to our Methodist ministry would mean giving up my job to go to seminary for four years, if accepted by the church. Earning no salary, I simply would have to stop helping my family. Also, according to the regulations then, I would have to wait seven years before being allowed to marry.

"In spite of all those apparently good reasons, the idea of offering myself for the ministry kept coming back to me with increasing force. At one point I felt utterly miserable as the battle in me raged. I was convinced that this was a call from God, but to respond positively to it seemed unreasonable. This period of uncertainty lasted about two months. I had decided to talk to no one about my problem; I had to fight the battle alone, only with God's help. My only recourse was prayer.

"One day all my doubts vanished; God's call must be given absolute priority. My heart overflowed with joy and a deep sense of peace pervaded my being. It was as if a veil had been drawn off. I wondered how I had hesitated for so long! I waited two weeks before talking to my pastor, as I wanted to be sure that this was not passing enthusiasm. But my conviction remained firm. I then spoke to him. He expressed his profound satisfaction, revealing to me that he had been praying that God might make me hear his special call; he had refrained from speaking to me about this lest I should have been influenced by him.

"I wrote to my family about my decision. My father sent me an angry and disturbing letter: his health was failing and he was counting on me to be the support of the family. I felt deeply sorry that he had not understood how God was calling me and that this had to be given precedence. He was to die two years later, but I had the great joy of seeing him change his opinion completely about my decision. Before going to seminary in Jamaica, after passing all the preliminary examinations, I invested most of my little savings in cattle for my family to make sure that they had a little capital to draw on, if need be. Some friends also thought that it was madness on my part to leave a good, promising job to become a penniless student and later a poorly paid minister. I knew they could not understand that I felt a deep sense of fulfillment enabling me to consider any alternative as incomparable.

"I spent three happy years at our seminary in Jamaica, West Indies. For my fourth and final year I was sent to England to attend the Handsworth Methodist Seminary and finish my work for the London University degree in theology. My years in seminary, both in Jamaica and England, were an enriching period in my life. My intellectual horizon broadened a good deal. I was anxious to take in as much as I could in order to be able to serve as well as possible my Lord, my church, and the people of Haiti.

"My active ministry in Haiti began in October, 1954, on my return from England. I began by serving in the Port-au-Prince circuit, being the assistant of the minister in charge, Rev. H. Ormonde McConnell. When he left for his furlough in Ireland a year later, I was put in charge of the circuit comprising then six churches. On top of that I was also responsible for the Cap-Haïtien circuit, about 160 miles from Port-au-Prince. This double charge was a heavy responsibility for a young minister, but with God's help I survived until Rev. McConnell came back. That experience taught me how inadequate were my personal resources for the demands made upon me; on the other hand, I experienced the truth that with God everything becomes possible. I discovered also that in Haiti a minister, beside being a preacher, a teacher, and a shepherd of the flock of Christ, is also called upon to show skills in accounting, in building, and in health care. Fortunately, I had had some practical training in those fields, and I was able to use my experience to good advantage.

"In the Cap-Haïtien circuit where I was stationed from 1956 to 1957, the church had a small dispensary housed in a thatch-covered hut in the heart of the countryside. It cared for people who came from miles around in search of treatment for their diseases. It was urgent to reconstruct something more adequate, however unpretentious it might be. The church having no money for that, with the help of an evangelist I was able to build with my own hands a modest but strong two-room dispensary. Every Thursday was clinic day. Cases which were beyond my understanding I referred to the hospital in town. In that dispensary I came face to face with the plight of the Haitian peasants who were easy prey to malaria, tuberculosis, intestinal worms, and malnutrition. Often they were sick because they were poor, and being sick they became even poorer. The children suffered most, and the sight of their bodies showing clear signs of malnutrition, the silent cries for help from their sad eyes, were constant challenges which could not be forgotten.

"In 1957 I was transferred to the Jérémie circuit. Shortly before leaving Cap-Haïtien I married the girl

 I had fallen in love with two years before. Now I could share my dreams and hopes, my defeats and victories with somebody very close to me. We went to Jérémie in August, 1957, knowing that a big job awaited us, the Jérémie circuit being the most widespread in our whole work in Haiti. It had one main church in town and over twenty churches dotting the countryside. Some of them were very difficult to reach. The two main roads into the countryside were dirt roads and, except for four-wheel-drive vehicles, were impassable in bad weather. Most of our small churches were pretty far from such main roads. To reach them one had to ride a horse for four, five, or six hours or walk on slippery tracks. But Jérémie was my hometown. I knew well a large section of the countryside; even more important, I knew the people's mentality. So I considered myself fortunate to be sent to that area.

"All kinds of urgent problems called for attention, so I had to be careful how I arranged my priorities. Preaching, journeys in jeeps, on horseback, or on foot, pastoral visitation of members, long files of people waiting on my veranda to see me were the ordinary program each week. Life was full of challenge, even if the work was backbreaking. My wife and myself were young and happy together, so we both felt that life was very fulfilling. We had the joy of welcoming our first baby, a girl whom we named Francoise, born in 1958.

"In the course of my numerous journeys and in my contact with the country folk, I was struck by their plight. The area had been devastated by hurricanes followed relentlessly by floods and droughts. Suffering caused by the serious economic situation was evident everywhere you went. Could I tell the people about God's love and not try to alleviate somehow their suffering? People in the countryside could hardly find money to buy even simple pieces of clothing. We managed once to get eighty-three bales of used clothing from Church World Service. After carrying out a methodical survey, we made hundreds of parcels with great care, to make sure that what was given suited the persons to whom it was given. My wife organized and directed the team of volunteer workers who helped us. That was a great success.

"This program did not please some local government leaders, because such a program showed too well that they themselves were not doing anything to help. But I quickly realized that one must strike at the very roots of such a situation if one is to change anything. At that time, churches in Haiti were not interested in the economic aspects of the people's lives. The accepted philosophy was that the role of the church was to help people find salvation for their souls in order that they might go to heaven. To me, the gospel spoke differently. It was for the whole person, for the whole of life, and for all people. Not many theories were yet being proposed about development. But then we thought that the best way to help people was not by handouts but by enabling them to produce more and better in order to gain more; they would then be able to break the vicious circle of poverty and disease.

"The peasant population had suffered a great deal from the political situation that had prevailed in the area in which I had escaped execution. Once the tension had decreased, it was urgent to develop the program we had started. But it needed to be enlarged in order that it might address itself to the health and educational situation as well. The peasants were practically without any medical care. Schools were so few and far between that the children remained illiterate. Such a situation could not leave us unmoved. With technical help from the right people, we presented plans for a rural rehabilitation project to the World Council of Churches in Geneva asking for financial backing. The project was endorsed by the WCC. Although we had planned an educational section, a medical section, a machine shop, and a wood section, as well as an agricultural and animal husbandry section, we were able to begin only with the last one due to a lack of personnel. In a matter of weeks something providential happened. We learned that a Swiss team of young Christians comprising a teacher, a nurse, and three agricultural technicians, led by a well-qualified agronomist, was available. They were an answer to prayer. We were thus able to open an outpatient clinic, a school, as well as give training in agriculture and animal husbandry. I was thrilled to have co-workers with the true Christian spirit. Very quickly the name of the project at Gebeau was known over a very wide area. This new responsibility made a heavy claim on my time, but it was a joy to be able to make an impact on the situation from the most important angles.

"This humble beginning in 1964 has grown to become for tens of thousands of peasants the source of their hope, a vital factor in their development. I have not been director of this project since 1968 when the church transferred me to Port-au-Prince, the capital city. But I rejoice to see the dream which God inspired become a concrete reality in the interest of the kingdom.

"The Methodist church has pioneered the movement for involving the church in the total life of the community. She should not shut herself in an ivory tower theologically or socially. She must proclaim the necessity and the possibility of the kingdom, its presence among us, even in the midst of our terrible human predicament, claiming all aspects of life for God in Christ. Thus our witness has been felt wherever there has been the necessity to meet great human need, or in various actions taken in order to liberate and develop people living at a subhuman level.

"In the light of my experience in Jérémie, it seemed absolutely necessary to me to affirm the vital importance of the work of the lay leaders and help them develop the gifts which they wanted to put at the service of the church. This led finally to the creation—a decision quite unprecedented in the life of the Caribbean Methodist districts—of a Department of Lay Leadership Training.

"This department could not be established immediately because of a lack of personnel. But when I was coming to the end of my five-year term as Chairman of the District, the church asked me to take a sabbatical year in order to prepare myself for the role of Director of the Lay Leadership program. I spent a most stimulating year at the Garrett-Evangelical Theological Seminary completing some studies. The sacrifice for myself and my family (my wife and children had to remain in Haiti) was hard but worthwhile. Moreover, thanks to the financial backing of the United Methodist Committee on Relief, this new department got its building and the necessary equipment to make it into a vital tool in the total operation of the church.

"Since my return to Haiti in July, 1976, I have been developing this program, organizing training seminars and courses, especially for the lay preachers who constitute the backbone of our work. I have also had to develop a curriculum for our Sunday schools, producing lesson notes both for teachers and children adapted to the Haitian situation. To back up this program we have been producing literature in French and Creole. Thus, we have developed our own printing shop which is meeting a great need in our church, producing teaching material as well for our sixty-five primary schools as well as serving other churches and educational institutions.

"So I am often on the road, I have to write a good deal, and I have had to become a printer. For the last two years our Synod has appointed me Superintendent of the Port-au-Prince Methodist circuit of sixteen churches, with pastoral responsibility for the Port-au-Prince congregation of over 900 members. I cannot complain of not having enough to do. I don't honestly remember any time in my ministry when I could have done so.

"In conclusion, there is so much to do and so little we can do! But how extraordinarily God can use our small loaves and fishes, what we have to offer, to do things 'wonderful in our eyes.'

"I am more grateful to God than I can say for calling me to the ministry. If I know that I have done God's will, I have the greatest possible reward. For the times when I have done my own will and failed God, I humbly ask for forgiveness and mercy."

The Lay Leadership Training Center is unique in the Caribbean and Central America. Through its doors have already passed hundreds of Haitian men and women who have claimed they have a ministry to their own people in the absence of a large number of trained clergy. Alain's spiritual secret is, "The Lord saved me for a great responsibility. We are all called to be part of God's answer."

Conclusion

When you enter a Buddhist temple you may encounter a serene Buddha such as the giant Gautama Buddha at Kamakura in Japan looking out across the landscape with attentive eyes and hands folded in repose. You then encounter in Kyoto, Buddhas with a thousand hands. Introduced into Japan from China in the ninth century, they are symbolic of the Buddha's ability to aid people in time of great peril whatever that need may be. The thousand-hand Buddha finds its origin in Hinduism in which many of the deities, such as Vishnu, Lakshmi, Narayana, Ganesan, and Ravana all have many hands.

Dr. Kosuke Koyama suggests that two normal hands do a better job in communicating love and mercy than a mystical idol of many hands.

Watch the long, tapered fingers of Dr. Antone Tarazi at work in a delicate operation in the hospital on the Mount of Olives; the stubby fingers of Toshihiro Takami demonstrating rice planting to a group of international students at Nishinasuno; or Esther Park pouring a cup of fragrant jasmine tea for you. Seeing these hands, you know all hands are not the same. However, these hands, along with Frank Field's and Alain Rocourt's, all have the same commitment. They are dedicated to God's ministry of healing, uplifting, comforting, teaching, persuading, and moving people. As Annie Johnson Flint says in her poem "The World's Bible":

> Christ has no hands but our hands
> To do His work today;
> He has no feet but our feet
> To lead men in His way.

In an earlier generation, Dwight L. Moody, the great evangelist, moved multitudes of people for God as Billy Graham has done in this generation. It is told of Moody as a young man that a friend seeing the great unrealized potential in him said to him, "Moody, the world has yet to see what would happen if someone gave himself wholly to God." Moody is reported to have said, "By the grace of God, I will be that person."

The lives of inspiration of the five men and women to whom you have been introduced are like pebbles cast into a still pond: their ripples spread on and on until they reach the bank. Many, many people around the world have been blessed by these ten hands which offer to all of us a challenge to give our hands and hearts to God to be a blessing to others.

William Gaither's lovely hymn "He Touched Me" gathers it all together for us:

> Shackled by a heavy burden,
> 'Neath a load of guilt and shame;
> Then the hand of Jesus touched me,
> And now I am no longer the same.
> He touched me, O, he touched me,
> and O, the joy that floods my soul;

> Something happened, and now I know,
> He touched me and made me whole.

"Then he led them out as far as Bethany, and lifting up his hands he blessed them" (Luke 24:50).

T4-ALI-565

The Carnaby Curse

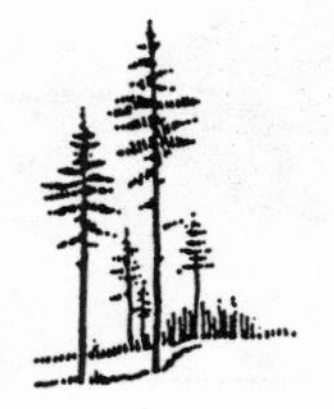

Also by Daoma Winston
in Thorndike Large Print

The Mayeroni Myth

This Large Print Book carries the Seal of Approval of N.A.V.H.

The Carnaby Curse

Daoma Winston

Thorndike Press • Thorndike, Maine

Library of Congress Cataloging in Publication Data:

Winston, Daoma, 1922-
The Carnaby curse / Daoma Winston.
p. cm.
ISBN 1-56054-515-1 (alk. paper : lg. print)
1. Large type books. I. Title.
[PS3545.I7612C37 1992] 92-24081
813'.54—dc20 CIP

All the characters in this book are fictitious. Any resemblance to actual persons, living or dead, is purely coincidental.

Thorndike Press Romance Series Large Print edition published in 1992 by arrangement with Jay Garon Brooke Associates.

Cover photo by Tom Knobloch.

This book is printed on acid-free, high opacity paper. ♾

The Carnaby Curse

Chapter 1

They had all been quiet since leaving Stoneleigh Village, and that was miles back.

Now the station wagon crept relentlessly around long, mist-hung curves. The tires hummed. There were faint splashing sounds from the windshield wipers. In their rhythmic whispers Megan Benson heard the echo of a name.

She huddled under the blue plaid blanket, and folded her small, thin hands in her lap. Her hair was a clear clean bronze, cut very short, and it curled in perfect symmetry to her head. Her eyes were dark brown, and wide-apart, and so large that it took a second glance to notice her straight narrow nose, her curved lips. She was twenty-four, but in that moment, she looked older. The shadows in her hollowed cheeks, under her big eyes, pressed years on her face, and her ringless fingers trembled as she braided them in her lap.

The windshield wipers echoed a name — Rory. Rory Ford. He was happy-go-lucky, she thought. Bright-eyed, and joyful. A perfect counter to her own more quiet and serious nature. And his easy laughter had covered some deep torment of which she had never been aware. She couldn't believe it. Yet his death was real.

Three weeks before she had been happily planning to be an autumn bride. She expected by that foggy night to be Mrs. Rory Ford, honeymooning with her husband in the clear sunlight of distant Bermuda. Instead she was Megan Benson riding slowly through the cold hills of Connecticut. Alone, though surrounded by what remained of her family. Alone, with her love once more taken from her.

She knew there was no use in trying to make sense out of what was senseless, no use in trying to find explanations when there were none. But she continued to ask herself if the facts of Rory's death were truly known. None had questioned them. None listened to her quiet protests. The unbelievable had to be believed. So she asked herself how she could have been blind to whatever it was that drove him to choose the grave instead of love, marriage and life.

She had not been able to weep, not when they told her, not in the days that followed. She drifted in numbed, choked, silence. But now, unaccountably, her eyes burned with tears. She drew a long, slow breath.

Instantly, her sister, Kristine, leaned towards her. "You're thinking of *him,* Megan." The light seventeen-year old voice spoke volumes of reproach.

Megan shook her head.

"But you have to forget. You promised me."

"Give me a little time." A forced grin touched Megan's lips, then faded.

Kristine's eyes were the color of clear amber, wide, expressive, intense. Her hair was pale brown, shot through with golden lights, and hung smooth and shining to her shoulders. Her mouth was small, very red. She was taller than Megan by several inches, and still had a touching adolescent awkwardness.

Megan knew that one day soon Kristine would fall in love. Then she would understand how Megan felt to be riding through a fog-smothered world, with the engagement ring Rory had given her locked away forever in her safety deposit box, and the dreams she had once had locked away forever in her heart. When that happened, Megan also knew, she would no longer be mother, father, sister, friend, to Kristine. She would no longer be the center of Kristine's life. But it hadn't happened yet.

Kristine said humbly, "I'm sorry, Megan."

"Don't be silly."

"Forgiven?"

"Forgiven." Megan turned to peer into the faint tunnel carved by the headlights. A warped and leafless tree floated out of the nothingness of mist, then drifted slowly away. She leaned back and closed her eyes.

She knew the road so well that she didn't have to see the rugged slabs of upright granite called Satan's Pillars that were on the left. She didn't have to see the lake, called Satan's Puddle on the right.

She had climbed the granite slabs, sailed the lake.

Arrows of pain drawn from old quivers shot through her.

The warped and leafless tree meant that they were almost there. Another mile or two, circling upward through the shrouded landscape, and she would be at Carnaby House.

She remembered the vow she had made when she left. The vow of a twenty-one-year-old girl, whose eyes were turned toward a happier future. She had said she would never return. Now, just three years later, she was going back. She knew now, with Rory dead, that where she was didn't matter. The Carnaby curse wasn't locked in Carnaby House. It had gone with her, followed her.

She shivered inside her black cashmere coat.

Kristine pressed closer to her. "Megan?"

She opened her eyes.

"Are you warm enough?" Smooth young hands patted the blanket they had tucked so solicitously around Megan before the trip began.

"I'm fine, Kristine."

Megan knew that Kristine had been frightened by the events of the past weeks, by the change she sensed in Kristine. Sweet, adoring, possessive, Kristine needed to be told constantly that the fixed center of her world had not crumbled.

Rory had said that Megan spoiled Kristine, but as he courted Megan, he had courted Kristine, too. It took him only a little while to prove that he could be brother to the younger sister, and husband to the elder.

That, Megan told herself, was another dream to be forgotten. She took Kristine's hand. "Don't worry, darling. It's you and me. We'll be okay together." She tried to force warmth, conviction, into the familiar words. Words said, with hope and love, so many times before. Yet she knew that Kristine heard the emptiness of the promise. She whispered, "Oh, Megan, please, I just want it to be like it used to be."

Celia Parr turned in the front seat. Her piled-high blonde waves glinted in the pale light. Her blue eyes were narrowed against her cigarette smoke. "Don't fuss so, Kristine.

Megan will be herself, her real self, as soon as she's home."

"Yes," Megan agreed. But that word, the word *home,* spoken so casually by Celia, echoed, tinged with bitterness in Megan's mind.

To her cousin Celia, to Terrence Parr, Celia's brother, at the wheel of the station wagon, even to Kristine, Carnaby House was home. But not to Megan. Never to her.

Celia demanded, "Terrence, can't you possibly go faster? This trip is taking years."

"Do you want to drive? If so, I'll stop, and you can take over. And when you've wrecked the wagon for me, you can buy me a new one. Which, as you well know, you can't afford."

"We're not talking about money," Celia retorted. "And, if we are, then what about you?"

The two of them were almost as alike as twins. Both were tall, slim, blond, with high cheekbones and pointed chins and self-indulgent mouths. But Terrence, twenty-six, and a year older than Celia, sometimes seemed to enjoy playing big brother.

Megan said hastily, "We're almost there now."

Terrence laughed. "And it's the same as always. Megan, the peacemaker, Kristine, the follower, and Celia, the . . ."

"Oh, do shut up, Terrence," Celia snapped.

Megan had the feeling that they had all somehow shifted backward in time. That she would have to live through those hurtful years in Carnaby House again.

She imagined that when they drove through the stone portals, her Aunt Vivian would be waiting. A tall woman in scented silk, her florid face disapproving, her pale blue eyes narrowed. She would look at Megan's father, say, "It's time you came home where you belong." And then, turning gimlet eyes on Megan, eight then, and tiny, almost collapsing under the weight of year-old Kristine. "So these are *her* daughters. I see." And behind her, the lights in the great entrance hall would be dim, and the suit of armor that stood, like a menacing warrior, at the foot of the wide staircase, would lean toward Megan, and she would cringe, reliving remembered terror.

"It's the right thing to do. I know it is," Celia said. "You had to get away, Megan. To be home. With your family again."

Megan nodded. But Celia's heart-shaped face, perfect in every detail, was turned toward Terrence. "There'll be a fire, and tea, and drinks if we want them. Budgie and Clyde will see to it all," Celia said.

A quick shudder rippled through Megan. Celia, Terrence, Kristine, each had their memories of Carnaby House. But their memories weren't hers.

Kristine asked, "Why don't you live there all the time, since you love the place so much?"

"There are reasons." Terrence paused, then laughed.

"Reasons," Celia said sharply. "One reason — money," she went on, "but, of course, neither of you would know anything about that."

Again Megan seemed to hear her Aunt Vivian, the mother of Celia and Terrence, speaking familiar words in a familiar voice.

The younger sister of Megan's father, Vivian had, on her parents' death, inherited Carnaby House, while Megan's father had been left a block of stocks, worth not much then, which became tremendously valuable over the years. Vivian married young, and well, but soon became widowed, receiving a fortune at that time. Yet, when her brother died suddenly in a fall, six years after bringing Kristine and Megan to Carnaby House, and left in trust for the girls what had become his considerable wealth, Vivian, appointed guardian by his will, soon made plain the bottomless depths of her jealousy.

Kristine had been too young to understand, and Megan had been the buffer that stood between Kristine and Vivian's jealousy of the girls. She had never mistreated the girls, but there had been no love, no joy, no peace, for Megan in Carnaby House.

Celia, no longer like her mother, said on a bubble of sweet laughter, "Not that I know how we'll manage to make expenses this time. But we will. We always do."

Megan wondered what had happened to the money her cousins inherited at their mother's death two years before. Vivian, of course, always lived extravagantly, and Celia and Terrence learned from her. Yet it was hard to imagine that everything was gone. Probably, Megan decided, they were simply talking poor, a practice that had become fashionable among the wealthy.

However, Megan said aloud, "I meant to speak to you about that. Naturally, as long as we're there, I'll take care of everything."

"Oh, nonsense, Megan." Terrence sounded annoyed. "We can't let you do that."

"But you wouldn't be going to Carnaby House if it weren't for me," Megan replied.

"Budgie and Clyde bless you. They hate being in those two little rooms of theirs with the rest of the place closed up. And we bless you, too," Celia retorted. "We only wanted the excuse." She smiled at Megan, narrowed eyes suddenly shining.

Megan tried to repress a tremor of shock at the words. Had Rory not died, she would be in Bermuda and she would never have been returning to Carnaby House.

Beside her, Kristine made a small sound of protest, as if she had read Megan's mind, or heard the sudden quick thud of her heart.

Celia, suddenly sober, muttered, "Oh, Megan, you know how I mean that, don't you? I just . . . well, you never let us do anything for you. And now . . ."

"Sister mine," Terrence drawled, "it's time you shut up."

"But Megan understands."

"Of course. She's known us long enough."

Then the stone portals leaned out of the fog.

Terrence swung the station wagon in a sharp right turn. The swinging headlights momentarily showed the blurred outlines of a low building, flashed on blank windows. Once the stables, it had been converted into a servants' cottage by Vivian in those days when she kept a large staff. It had been unused, Megan knew, for many years.

"Look," Terrence murmured, awe in his voice.

High on the ridge to which the road curved, dim and diffused yellow light floated above the moving mists. Light seemed to spill from the emptiness of the shrouded sky. Beyond it, the land sloped down to the bluffs that hung over Satan's Puddle. Dread was a cold hard kernel in Megan's chest. They were nearly there. . . .

Chapter 2

She huddled in the blanket that circled her, remembering how chilly it had been just two days before.

Kristine, Celia, and Terrence had come in together, their faces full of secrets, after what had obviously been a council of war.

Celia paced the beige rug in long swinging strides. Terrence took a vice-presidential seat behind the mahogany desk. Kristine sat on the floor beside Megan, a comforting warmth against her legs.

Megan knew what they saw when they looked at her. She didn't really care that her hair was unbrushed, her eyes swollen from lack of sleep, her black dress so big on her that it looked like an unaltered hand-me-down.

"Megan," Celia said, "we've been talking about you. We're worried. It's terrible, but you have to go on. I know Rory would want that."

She wondered what they expected of her. She *was* going on. She was alive, while Rory was dead.

Celia sighed. "Listen, Megan, you ought to

get away from here. You need a change, rest, time to pull yourself together. So we'll re-open Carnaby House. We'll all go up there. Budgie and Clyde will take care of us the way they used to."

"Would you do it for me?" Kristine pleaded, looking at Megan through a veil of shining hair. "For me?"

Megan thought of Rory gone. His warm smile, easy laughter. Rory, to whom she had belonged too briefly.

The day that it happened she had been angry. Kristine, having promised to meet her for a final fitting of her maid of honor gown, left word at the couturier's that she had decided, instead, to go to the movies, and would see Megan at home. Megan was angry at that, and then even angrier when she found that the train of her white satin bridal dress was too long to be gracefully managed. Two days before the wedding she burned, fumed and wept. A ridiculous excess of emotion, but she couldn't help it. When she finally got home, a policeman broke the horrible news — Rory was dead.

That day, while Kristine sat in the movies, while Megan wept over her bridal gown, Rory loaded one of his heirloom pistols, and pressed its muzzle to his chest, and killed himself.

His family came and took him home for

burial. They didn't need her. Rory's older brother, whom she had never met, was returning from overseas. He could do more to help his parents than she could.

She withdrew into the beige and brown apartment, and spent the day asking herself how she had failed Rory.

"Please," Kristine begged. "It would be so wonderful . . . for me, Megan?"

Megan nodded. "All right, if that's what you want."

They gave her no time to reconsider.

Celia immediately called Budgie and Clyde to make the arrangements.

Kristine gathered her records, books and clothes.

They spent two frantic days closing the apartment, packing.

Now the station wagon crept up the curving road through the drifting mist. Megan watched the diffused yellow light grow stronger. She told herself that it didn't matter where she was. Rory, like the others she once loved, had died. The curse was not locked within the thick walls of Carnaby House.

But as the station wagon drifted to a stop before the wide stone steps, the hard kernel of dread in her chest melted and ran through her in an icy wave. Lips numb, mouth dry, she whispered, "No, no."

Chapter 3

The house, originally two stories high and square, had been built by one of the 19th century Bensons. His heirs had added wings and porches, each to his own taste. Now Carnaby had carved balustrades, cornices and pointed arches. Its stone walls were sooty gray. Its wooden trim weathered silver. It seemed to float above the ridge in a clutch of fog, anchored to earth only by the steps that led to its huge front door.

It was a steep flight, broken at its center by a wide landing which was enclosed on each side by stone planters set with carefully trimmed boxwood.

There, on an icy night, when Megan was fourteen and Kristine was seven, their father had fallen. He was unconscious when Clyde found him amid the shards of a broken vase that he had been carrying out-of-doors for no reason. He died the next morning of a skull fracture. But he had asked to see Kristine. "He wanted to see Kristine," Vivian told Megan, in a voice syrupy with satisfaction. "Kristine. But, of course. I couldn't . . . she *is* so young."

He had planned a birthday trip for Megan, a flight to London for two weeks. Kristine, he said, was the baby. Her turn would come later. The trip became a long ride to the cemetery.

"We're home," Celia said now.

"The way we used to be," Kristine whispered, drawing the blanket from around Megan, leaving her wrapped in a chill that had nothing to do with the cold misty night.

"Let's go in. Clyde can get the stuff," Terrence said.

The others got out, chattering happily. Megan followed. She paused at the foot of the stairs. Kristine nudged her. "Come on."

"Did the trip tire you?" Terrence asked, a hand at her elbow.

Megan shook her head, unable to speak. Arrows of pain from the old quiver lanced into her. Between the loss of her father and the loss of Rory there had been another.

With Terrence on one side of her, Kristine on the other, she raised her haggard face to the blowing mist. But it had become a sweet, warm sun, and she was seventeen again. Seventeen, in love for the first time, certain it would last forever. The huge house full of moldering antiques, a prison from which the only escape was the elopement she and Bob planned in joyful whispers as they climbed Satan's Pillars and sailed Satan's Puddle. She was on the wide stone stairs when gray-faced Clyde came around the house and passed her without a glance or word, and moments later, Budgie stumbled out whispering that Bob was dead. "It's a curse," she said, "a curse on this house."

It was true, Megan knew. The curse of Carnaby meant death to those she loved. She had vowed then to leave Carnaby House as soon as she could. When she turned twenty-one, and became her own mistress, she took Kristine, and moved to the city. Vivian did not protest. She gave Megan a detailed accounting of the estate, to which Megan paid no attention, and promptly washed her hands of the girls. It was as if the thirteen years they had lived with her had never been. . . .

Celia had run ahead. But before she reached it, the wide door was flung back. Budgie stood there waiting, a great shapeless silhouette against the dim light.

Megan took a long slow breath. She told herself that there was no longer anything to fear from Carnaby House.

As she reached the threshold and was taken into Budgie's arms, the fear was there; vague and uneasy, as unsubstantial as the mist that clung to the gray stone walls — but just as real.

"Megan, my poor child," Budgie said. "We're so sad for you."

Budgie was ageless. She had been old when Megan first saw her, growing older through Megan's childhood. She hadn't changed: big and homely, her voice perpetually hoarse. She wore her iron-gray hair wrapped around her head in perfect braids that never wisped or frayed. She wore her simple black silk dress as if it were a uniform. Her eyes were as gray as Satan's Puddle on a stormy day.

Clyde, her husband, standing behind her, was ageless too. He nodded the quick nervous nod that Megan recognized as nothing more than a habit with him. He was huge, even larger than Budgie, and ashen-faced and gaunt. There were great ravines in his cheeks, and black hollows under eyes . . . black as coal.

They had been Megan's allies in the house that had never seemed home to her.

She went to Clyde, touched his wrinkled cheek.

"I'm sorry," he rumbled.

"That's enough of that," Celia cried. "We brought her home to forget."

Megan stood still, looking around the great hall. Everything was as she remembered it. The huge crystal chandelier cast a peculiar play of shadows on the white walls where bridles and bits were hung between crossed swords in an incongruous display. The empty suit of armor, lance under one arm, leaned against the mahogany bannister of the wide curving stairway that led upward into the darkness of the second floor.

"Dinner in an hour," Clyde said. "The same rooms are all ready for you if you want to go up first. Tea and drinks in the drawing room. I'll get your luggage in."

"Down in a minute," Kristine told Megan, and then to Clyde, "be careful of my records." She followed Celia and Terrence up the steps, chattering happily at them.

Budgie touched a switch, and beyond the curve of the stairs, the second floor chandelier spilled a pale pink glow on the carved bannisters. She turned to Megan. "I'll see to dinner," and Megan was left alone.

She went into the drawing room. Fear, a second self, went with her. She looked at the familiar panelled walls, old and dark with the years, absorbed with secrets. The huge copper tray, souvenir of some long-ago Benson's North African trip, hung in its accustomed place above the sofa. The tiny teak tables were, as always before, set beside the deep leather chairs.

Budgie and Clyde had done their work well in little time. There was a fire, as Celia had predicted. The room was clean and warm, and from somewhere they had gotten great masses of yellow and copper chrysanthemums and set them about in tall vases. Water for tea simmered in its pot on an electric tray. The ice bucket was ready, decanters at its side.

Megan sighed, looked into the fire. The flames built swiftly changing images. Her father's face, Rory's and Bob's. She gasped, stumbled to the door.

Budgie was there. "Megan?"

"I'll go up now. I want to rest," Megan said weakly.

What she really wanted was to be alone. In the past three weeks she had had precious little privacy. Kristine had spent every moment with her since learning of Rory's death. Celia and Terrence had come and gone with surprising frequency, considering that Megan had rarely seen them before.

Budgie trailed her up the stairs, and Kristine met her in the pink-lit hall and inquired, "What's wrong, Megan?"

"Nothing, darling. Relax." She heard the touch of impatience in Kristine's voice, forced a smile, saying, "I guess I *am* a little tired."

Megan went ahead of them, down the pink-lit hall that stretched endlessly before her to her old room.

It had been untouched in the years since

she left it. The heavy maroon brocade hung at the big windows. The maroon canopy threw a black shadow over the big four-poster bed.

Kristine and Budgie watched her as she went from lamp to lamp, opening switches until the room was flooded with rose-colored light.

Budgie said, "Kristine, run down and tell Clyde that Megan will have her dinner on a tray."

"I'm not hungry. Never mind, Kristine."

"But you have to eat, Megan. For me," she pleaded.

"Go on," Budgie said.

Kristine grinned. "I recognize that tone, Megan. You better do what Budgie says."

Megan waited until Kristine had gone then told Budgie, "I'm too old to be taken care of now."

"Twenty-four?" Budgie laughed. "It doesn't seem old to me."

"And I shouldn't have come back."

"Why not?"

"You know why, Budgie." Budgie remembered the day on the steps, remembered telling her that Bob was dead. First her father, then Bob, now Rory. . . .

A wary look welled into Budgie's eyes. She said, "You told me you were all grown up." She went to the bed, folded back its pink satin spread, plumped the pillows, turned the quilt down. "You'll feel better after a nap."

The door clicked open. Megan turned quickly.

It was Clyde, bringing in her suitcases. "I thought you'd need these now. Dinner in a little while." Megan nodded her thanks.

When he had gone, Budgie unpacked.

Megan put on a green gown, and laid down on the sheets.

"You're a lot thinner," Budgie said. "And if I guess right by this . . ." She held up the black dress Megan had just taken off, ". . . you're in mourning."

Megan nodded.

"You mustn't. It's not good for you, nor for Kristine. You ought to give it up. It doesn't help."

"I will," Megan said.

She had worn black for herself, not for a public display of mourning. There was no need to oppress the others with what was her loss — only hers.

"Thank you." Budgie smiled, but the wary look was back in her eyes. "Nap now."

When she had gone, Megan tried to relax against the pillows. She stared into the circles of rose-colored light, and listened to the soft sounds of the old house. They seemed to whisper satisfaction. She had returned. Its victim had come back.

Chapter 4

The room was cold. She drew the quilt closer, knowing it wouldn't help. The cold was a part of Carnaby House. . . .

Kristine was ten that summer, a demanding ten. She dogged Megan's footsteps with a devotion that became a burden, Megan accepting only because she adored Kristine. But even with Kristine, Megan was lonely, and seventeen is a rebellious year. Celia and Terrence had both been away to school, and spent their vacation months visiting friends throughout the state. Vivian had decided that Megan must stay at home and go to school in Stoneleigh Village, since Kristine could not bear a long separation. Bob sailed across Satan's Puddle to fill the empty days with laughter and love. He and Megan climbed Satan's Pillars together, with Kristine trailing them, swam in the lake, with Kristine following, graceful as a small seal. There were some nights, when Kristine finally slept, that the two of them were alone under the summer stars.

The dreams of seventeen are sweet until they turn into nightmare. Her nightmare came on a bright day when Bob left her and went down to Satan's Puddle to show Kristine a shell he'd found. Waving goodbye, she'd later told Megan, he sailed away. A few hours later, Clyde came, and Budgie took Megan into her arms, held her on the wide stone steps where she and Bob had planned their elopement, and said, "It's a curse on this house."

Budgie had named it. Yet when Megan told her, "I know. I know. Anyone I need, anyone I love will die," Budgie had looked frightened and said, "Megan, that's strange and wild talk. Don't let your Aunt Vivian hear you say that!"

Megan never spoke of it again. But as soon as she could, she took Kristine and fled Carnaby House.

But Rory had died, too. She knew that the curse lay upon her still. Strange and wild thoughts, Budgie would say.

Megan clenched her fists at her temples. Was she going mad? Had she always been mad? Was there a curse that she must accept, believe in? Or had Rory killed himself because . . . because of something in her?

She closed her eyes against the quick burn of tears. The cold walls of Carnaby House claimed her. She had to face what she would never face before. Her love for Rory had been no more than need to belong to someone, a need for someone to give meaning to her in an empty world. Had he known, suspected, those reservations within her? Had he killed himself rather than try to build a marriage on those terms?

She had thought, when Celia and Terrence talked about it, when Kristine pleaded, that it didn't matter where she was. But now, once again, Megan wished that she hadn't allowed herself to be persuaded. She wished she hadn't returned to Carnaby House.

It would have been better to live with her illusions, to wear mourning, and go numbly through the empty hours, than to know that Rory had died for nothing . . .

"Do you have a headache?" Kristine asked softly.

She was beside the bed, her long hair shining in the lamp light, her wide amber eyes anxious. "Megan, why are you doing that?"

Megan took her fists from her temples. She hadn't heard Kristine come in. "No," she said. "I'm all right."

"But the way you look . . ."

"Darling, don't worry about me."

"I'll keep you company." Kristine threw herself on the bed, snuggled close to Megan. "I shouldn't have left you alone. I went exploring. And it's all the same. Did you want me here?"

"I was thinking."

"About what?"

But Megan shrugged, forcing a smile.

There was a tap at the door, and it opened. Clyde came in with a big tray almost hidden in his huge hands. "Megan, you should be resting."

"I'm keeping her company," Kristine told him.

Clyde grunted. He set the tray before Megan. "Budgie says you're to eat it all."

"Want some?" she asked Kristine.

"I'm starving." Kristine put a hand out, but withdrew it at Clyde's disapproving look. "I guess not, thanks."

The ravines in his gray cheeks became dimples with his approving grin.

Megan made a tunnel in the mashed potatoes, shredded the roast chicken and splashed coffee in the saucer.

Clyde finally took the tray away.

Soon Celia came in. She had changed from her beige suit to a pale blue slack suit. Her piled-high blonde hair gleamed in the lamp light. "Why, there you are," she said, her pale blue eyes glowing. "I couldn't imagine where you'd gone, Megan. Terrence suggested you'd floated away in the mists. It's an awful night and getting worse, if you could believe it."

"Budgie persuaded me to rest," Megan told her.

"A good idea." Celia turned her glowing

eyes on Kristine. "Now, sweetie, you mustn't hang about. Megan wants to rest. Come along with me. We'll have dinner and see about the pool table."

"Which is in a terrible state of repair," Terrence told her, poking his head in the door. "Is this a hen party? Or may a mere male join you?"

"Come in," Kristine said.

He grinned. "All settled, Megan? Comfortable? Anything I can do?"

"I'm fine," she told him.

Celia demanded, "Why don't you fix the pool table?"

"Why don't you?" he retorted.

"I'm too tired," she said sweetly.

"Don't tell me your troubles. I've got troubles of my own."

Money again, Megan thought, listening as they bickered in light laughter-filled voices.

They left with Kristine. "I'll be back," she promised. "And I'm right next door, the way I used to be, Megan. If you want me, just give a yell."

Megan sighed when the door had closed behind them. The effort to talk, be calm and be her normal self seemed more than she had strength for. It was easier to be alone.

Listening to the small sounds of the old house, sensing the threat remembered from her childhood, she sank slowly into sleep, the rose-colored lamp light a distant dawn against her closed eye lids . . .

The dream formed slowly. Sun and shadows in a garden of roses. Sun and shadows on a familiar shore. Kristine waved a small hand. Rippling water rolled back, and a dark, shapeless thing reached out, reached out for her. Someone screamed, a thin and distant sound.

Megan came up out of sleep, her heart beating too quickly, breath gone, throat raw. The scream continued, closer now, suddenly not a dream, but real and echoing.

Budgie stood over her. For a terrible moment, they stared at each other. "A nightmare, Megan?" Budgie asked finally.

Megan nodded, her throat aching. She knew that the thin and distant voice, suddenly real, had been her own.

Budgie reached out to turn off the lamps.

"Leave them on. I don't want to be in the dark," Megan said.

"At twenty-four years old!"

"I'm going away tomorrow," Megan said. She had decided, in that moment, what she must do.

Budgie eyed her then. "You can't run forever, Megan." When Megan didn't answer, Budgie went on, "Sleep on it, everything will be different in the morning."

After she had gone, Megan dozed. Some time later, when the door opened, she awakened.

Kristine whispered, "Asleep, Megan?"

But Megan didn't move.

Terrence said, "Hush, don't disturb her."

"But she didn't say good night," Kristine protested. "She always says good night."

"Grow up," Terrence retorted.

"You hush," Kristine cried. "She belongs to me!"

Slowly, the rose-colored lights receded as the lamps clicked off. Megan heard Terrence say, "Now for heavens' sake, leave her be for a change, Kristine."

Chapter 5

Megan came slowly, unwillingly out of sleep. There were moments before she remembered where she was, but they soon ended, and she longed for sleep again.

The house was wrapped in silence, yet she sensed an unheard, unseen, threat. It was as if some evil had always been there, waiting to claim her.

She got out of bed and went to the window. She opened the maroon drapes and stared wide-eyed into thick white emptiness.

Terrence had been wrong. The fog had not lifted. He would not sail that day on Satan's Puddle. The lake lay shrouded below the bluffs, and the world outside seemed gone. It was as if Carnaby House had drifted away from the ridge on which it had stood for so many years, drifted away on a cotton cloud.

Megan reminded herself that she was going home. The closed apartment could be reopened. Terrence could drive her back.

With a quick knock, Budgie opened the door and came in. "You'll catch cold. Hop into bed, Megan. I've brought you coffee."

"I want to leave early."

"You can have coffee, can't you?"

"I suppose." Megan got into bed reluctantly. She thought that the sooner she was gone the better.

Budgie watched as she drank the strong, hot coffee.

Kristine bounded in. "I thought I heard you talking." And to Budgie, "You didn't bring me *my* coffee."

"You can eat downstairs with the others," Budgie told her.

"But I want to eat with Megan."

"It's too much trouble for Budgie and Clyde," Megan said quickly.

But Budgie said she would bring Kristine's breakfast along with Megan's, and she left.

Kristine curled up on the bed, her amber eyes on Megan's face. "You're better already."

"I want to go home," Megan told her. "This isn't going to be any good."

"It's as if we're alone now. In our own little world," Kristine murmured.

Megan said, "I'm sorry, darling. Truly, but. . . ."

"We don't need anybody but us, do we, Megan?" Kristine's amber eyes were too bright, too anxious.

Megan said gently, "Kristine, I do really

want to go home."

"It's my fault, isn't it?"

"Yours?"

"That you hate it here."

"No. It has nothing at all to do with you, darling."

"Then why, Megan, why?"

But Megan didn't know how to explain. She had always been the buffer between Kristine and their aunt, between Kristine and Carnaby House. She had tried to give Kristine the sense of security, comfort and joy she had never felt herself.

"It *is* my fault," Kristine sighed. "I made you come."

She began the sweet blackmail, and Celia and Terrence continued it.

The cousins came in after breakfast, both tall and blond, as alike as twins.

Terrence had a vase full of chrysanthemums. He grinned. "Budgie says you're to stay in bed today, so I brought you these."

"Didn't she tell you that I want to go back?" Megan asked.

"Really, what is this?" His blond brows drew down. "Don't joke now."

And Celia cried, "Oh nonsense, you're not a child."

"What have we done?" Terrence demanded. "Or what haven't we done?"

"Please tell us," Celia begged, "we want to help."

Their pale blue eyes watched Megan anxiously while Kristine waited in silent entreaty.

It was easier to give in than to argue, so she gave in. As earlier she gave in when Budgie told her she must stay in bed.

She dozed, daydreamed and read a little through two slow days. Kristine stayed by her side, as if afraid that if she turned her back, Megan would disappear into the fog that clung to the ridge.

But Megan saw the young girl's bright smile begin to dim, saw the sullen shadow grow in her amber eyes, and knew that Kristine was beginning to understand that the particular cure she had counted on was not working. "You're thinking of *him,*" she often told Megan.

Terrence brought more flowers, a box of candy, books, and stopped to chat. Celia came and went, trailing sweet perfume, and laughter that faded only when she bickered with her brother about money.

Budgie and Clyde lavished attention on Megan, yet she sensed a strange caution behind it, and knew that they were watching her, but didn't know why.

Megan told Budgie that she intended to support the house as long as she and Kristine were there.

"Why should you do that? You're a guest here now."

"I prefer to, Budgie."

She shrugged, but looked relieved when Megan wrote out a check.

Seeing that, Megan asked, "Budgie, what do you suppose is wrong? Celia and Terrence should be very well fixed."

"Ask her how she spends it. Ask Terrence." Budgie's lips turned down in contempt.

"How do you and Clyde manage when the house is closed?"

"We do. There's no other place for us, Megan."

"Why, Budgie, don't they send you anything?"

"When they remember."

"I see," Megan said thoughtfully.

"Not that I should have told you. It's not your responsibility."

But it was, Megan thought, when Budgie had gone. There had to be some way to make sure that the two old people had an adequate income.

"You're thinking of *him* again," Kristine said sullenly, slamming the door shut.

Megan forced herself to smile. "Not that time, darling."

Poor Kristine. She wouldn't say Rory's name any more. She wanted to forget that he had ever existed.

"It is better now, isn't it?" Kristine demanded.

Megan agreed. Though her thoughts still made the same circle, though she dreamed still of the Carnaby curse, though fear, like a second self, lay with her while she lay in bed.

"I just want it to be the way it used to be," Kristine mumbled.

"Give me time, darling," Megan told her, knowing she had said the same thing before.

Celia came striding in. "I've been out-of-doors. And it's lovely. All thick and wet and white. Like snow hanging over us, but not really cold." She hunched over the edge of the bed, her blue eyes studying Megan. "My goodness, why don't you comb your hair? Kristine, be a sweetie, get your sister's make-up and brush, and bring it here."

"It doesn't matter," Megan said.

"Do you like looking like a dragged-in cat?"

"There's nobody here."

"Nobody? Well, really, Megan." Celia made a pretense at a haughty face. "I am somebody. And Kristine is. And we have to look at you. Even if you don't look at yourself. And then, what about Terrence? He just adores you, and . . ."

"Terrence is used to seeing me at my worst."

"But he *is* a man. Or hadn't you noticed?"

As if on cue, Terrence banged on the door, threw it open.

"Who's taking my name in vain?" he demanded.

"We all are." Kristine giggled. "Celia just said you are a man."

"We won't argue." He grinned at Megan. "I have decided on a surprise." He turned to Celia and Kristine. "Girls, a trip to Stoneleigh Village?"

"I'll stay here," Kristine told him.

"You won't. You need some air."

"Is there really going to be a surprise?"

"Come and find out."

"If you're going to spend money, Terrence, it better be your own," Celia told him.

"We'll argue about it later," he laughed.

When they had gone, Megan got up. She turned on all the lamps. Rose-colored light hid the gray shadows. She was at the window when Budgie came in.

"You want to be careful, Megan. You can brood yourself into . . . into . . ."

Megan waited.

Budgie said lamely, "Well, you can make yourself sick."

"It's just been a little over three weeks."

"I know. Only you want to be careful, Megan. So much self-indulgence." Budgie's mouth turned down. "So much giving in. What about Kristine? Oughtn't you to make some effort?"

Megan went back to bed.

Budgie straightened the quilt. Her big hands were gentle, more gentle than Megan could have imagined possible, if she hadn't known that touch from years before.

"And the brooding . . ." Budgie gave her a wary look. "I tell you, it's dangerous, Megan."

"What are you talking about?"

She shrugged.

Megan knew there was no use in pursuing it. Budgie had said what she wanted to say and would add no more to it unless she changed her mind. Megan recognized the firm line of those unpainted lips, the firm set of those squared shoulders.

She sighed, closed her eyes.

Budgie said, "You better get up for dinner tonight." And then, "You like hiding away in here too much."

"You suggested it yourself."

"You needed the rest. I didn't plan for you to be up here forever."

"Two days isn't forever, Budgie."

"It can be a habit." She shook her head.

"And look at you!"

"You and Celia!"

"Somebody has to take you in hand."

Budgie, they all were right, Megan thought, as she dressed that evening. She had known loss and death too often and too intimately to abandon herself in the arms of a grief that proved a burden to others. She had learned before to carry her sorrow privately. She determined to do it once more. She wouldn't give in. Not to sorrow, not to fear.

She wore a blue dress that was full at the hem and narrow at the waist. She brushed her bronze hair into a smooth cap and put on makeup. Her big brown eyes stared at her out of the mirror, bewildered and frightened as she clipped on the tiny sapphire earrings that had belonged to her mother.

Kristine said, "It doesn't seem fair. I wish I could remember her."

"I hardly do myself," Megan answered, knowing that was the reply Kristine wanted.

Megan did remember their mother. A small woman with short bronze curls, big brown eyes and a gay laugh. She had come home from the hospital with Kristine and put the baby in Megan's lap saying, "Your sister, darling. Take care of her." Megan had looked into the rose-petal face, whispering, "Isn't she beautiful?" She remembered that and remembered that their mother had grown smaller over the next months, the sweet laughter stilled, and finally, she had gone away. Kristine was a year old when their mother died.

"But still," Kristine said wistfully, "I ought to have some memories."

Megan found, when ready to go down, that the two days in bed had melted away her strength. It took effort for her to walk to the door. She paused to rest.

"What's wrong?" Kristine demanded.

"Nothing, darling." Megan forced herself to smile. "I got tired from resting."

"But you won't change your mind?"

"Oh, no."

Later she wished she had.

They were in the drawing room. The fire danced on the hearth. She saw faces in the flames again. Her father, Rory; her father, Bob. She closed her eyes against them, and Budgie demanded, "Megan, what *is* the matter with you?"

Terrence made a great to-do about opening a magnum of champagne. "Your surprise," he said. "With this we drink to your good health, Megan. To your good future."

"To your happiness," Celia finished, laughing softly.

Megan thanked them, smiled, sipped the

bubbly wine, and wished that she were miles away.

Kristine, sitting close beside her on the sofa, whispered, "This is how it should be, Megan. Always. Always."

Megan supposed she should be grateful for their attempts to mend her sagging spirits, even though they were not yet ready to be mended, even though their too obvious concern somehow made her own efforts to forget more difficult. She was immediately ashamed of that thought.

But she felt the walls close in. Her heart began to beat in slow awful strokes. She stared blindly at the fire until Budgie called them all to dinner.

Afterwards, when they had settled before the television set, she slipped out of the darkened room. She found her coat in the great hallway and put it on, letting herself out of the house.

The cocoon of fog still lay on the ridge. But through the vague, wavery shapes of the trees, she saw a faint shimmer of light from the stables. She watched it, wondering why Clyde could have gone there, and then, as she picked her way down the wide stone steps, she forgot the stables and Clyde.

She was remembering Terrence's and Celia's toast. They had meant well. But with

Rory gone she had no future. Her life was as empty as the fog-bound world.

She stumbled, and almost fell, and caught herself. She thought of Rory, but her unwilling feet took her to the bluff above Satan's Puddle. She crouched there, shivering inside her heavy coat.

From below, she heard faint rippling sounds breaking on the rocks where Bob's body had been found seven years before.

That day had been full of sunlight with the sky unbelievably blue and the slope green with summer growth. Kristine appeared suddenly on the bluffs. She wore a pink sun suit. Her long hair blew in the warm breeze. "It was a beautiful shell," she cried. "Bob's going to save it for me. He waved goodbye and yelled that he'd be back." And a few hours later, Clyde found him bruised by the rocks.

Now there was nothing but a heavy cloud of white, a rustle of wind in the leafless maples. Megan crouched on the bluff, bent her head, and wept. Finally, the hot tears stopped, and the fog had broken into trailing wraiths, smoke-like figures drifting before her stinging eyes.

Below her, she saw the ripple of night-dark water that was Satan's Puddle. Around her she saw the slim silhouettes of bare trees. She straightened up, and as she did, she realized that she wasn't alone.

Someone was watching her from a ridge of rock. A dark shadow in the broken fog. A motionless figure, oddly intent, oddly threatening where no figure ought to be.

She scrambled to her feet.

The black hunched figure shifted, shifted like something out of her dreams.

Thought and sense deserted her. She became a puppet animated by irrational terror. She turned and fled.

Chapter 6

She ran pursued by the sounds of a hoarse call and the quick clatter of spinning pebbles.

The broken mist reformed, thick and blinding, reaching for her.

Ahead, high on the slope, was the diffused yellow light of the house. It seemed to recede as she raced toward its dubious safety.

A loose limb of a tree caught her and slowed her pace. She fell, and before she could get to her feet, the thudding sounds were on her, footsteps as loud as thunder. Fingers brushed her hair.

She rolled clumsily, fighting quick warm hands that sought to hold her. She struggled, terror-stricken, subdued and powerless. She lay still within the steel-like circle of arms, staring wide-eyed and waiting into a stranger's face.

He said, his voice very deep, "I didn't mean to scare you. Why did you run?"

For one fleeting instant she felt a peculiar joy. It faded so swiftly it might never have touched her.

Struggling against the arms that held her, she cried, "Let me go."

"Are you sure you're all right now?"

"Oh, yes. Just let me go."

The arms fell away from her.

She scrambled to her feet.

"Did I hurt you?"

"But who are you? What do you want? What are you doing here?" she demanded.

His laugh was soft. "All at once? Just like that?"

She turned, limping toward the light on the ridge. He took her arm. "Better let me help you."

"Who are you?"

He handed her a handkerchief. "You can use this."

She accepted it and mumbled her thanks. She daubed the dirt on her face repeating, "But what do you want?"

"Why, nothing. I'm Liam Judge. I moved into the stables today."

"The stables?" She remembered the light she had seen there earlier.

"Didn't the Parrs tell you? I'm the new tenant. The Johnstones recommended this place to me. They didn't say anyone would be here, though."

"We just decided to come a week or so ago."

He was much taller than she, and he had to bend his head to speak to her.

"I was walking around," he went on. "Making myself at home. I saw you . . . I mean at the bluffs, and I . . ."

"You didn't have to stand and watch me."

"I couldn't help but wonder what was wrong." He moved slowly beside her, a hand at her elbow.

She wished that he wouldn't touch her. "It isn't pleasant," she said, "to find oneself being stared at. You nearly frightened me out of my wits."

"I thought for a few seconds that I really had."

"I don't think it's funny," she said coldly.

"I didn't mean to be."

She stumbled and his fingers tightened on her arm.

"You needn't walk me back," she said.

"I'd rather."

It seemed useless to argue. She was suddenly exhausted, chilled. She let him lead her up the slope to the stone steps. There, she stopped. "I didn't introduce myself, Mr. Judge. I'm Megan Benson."

"*You* are?" There was an odd emphasis in his deep voice.

She heard it and wondered. "Yes," she said. "*I* am."

He nodded and gave her a smile.

In the dim yellow light from the house, she suddenly saw his features, the shape of his head, the expression of his eyes for the first time.

And she wondered if it were the first time. She had a fleeting sense of familiarity, a faint recognition almost instantly gone, gone but still remembered.

His deep-set eyes were very dark, narrowed and serious. They looked down at her questioningly. His dark hair was close-cropped and tousled. His chin was squared under a long compressed mouth that was grim in repose. He wore wrinkled chino trousers and a matching windbreaker, an outfit that emphasized the lean wide-shouldered body.

Responding to her long slow stare, he said, "I'm not such a monster as all that, am I?"

She shook her head, turned to go inside.

"Wait a minute."

His big hands touched her hair and smoothed the bronze curls.

Once again she felt a peculiar joy, but it swiftly died in the sudden sinking of her heart. It was the same as when she first saw him, a hunched shadow in the broken mist.

She shrank away from him. "Don't, don't."

"If you could see yourself," he said lightly, but his dark eyes were intent and watchful.

"It doesn't matter." But she looked down at her coat. It had a long streak of mud down the front. Bits of dried leaves clung to the dark wool. She shrugged and once more turned to go inside.

He said, "I'm not dressed for visiting, but now that I'm here perhaps I could step in and introduce myself to the Parrs."

"If you like," she unwillingly agreed.

"I don't want to impose, of course."

She very nearly said, 'Then don't.' but managed to stop herself in time. She knew that he understood. There was grim amusement in his eyes.

When she opened the heavy door, Kristine came out of the drawing room. "Oh, there you are, Megan. We were worried to death. Where did you go? Why didn't you tell us." She stopped, finally out of breath, and noticed Liam. A flush came up on her cheeks and her amber eyes widened. "I'm sorry. I didn't know anybody was with you. And when you went out like that . . ." She paused uncertainly, and Budgie, appearing behind her, put a hand on her shoulder.

Clyde towered over them both, his gaunt gray face full of curiosity.

Megan made the introductions quickly.

Clyde rumbled, "Then you're the one Celia told me about. I hope the place is comfortable."

"It's fine," Liam assured him.

Megan slipped out of her coat, and Budgie,

taking it from her with a click of disapproval, hung it away.

Liam, instead of leaving, unzipped his windbreaker.

"Come in and meet Celia and Terrence," Kristine cried.

As they crossed the hall, Megan saw Liam look around, quick dark glances touching the crossed swords, the bridles and bits on the wall, sliding toward the suit of armor at the foot of the stairs. Then he turned to look at her. She hurried ahead of him.

Celia was curled on the floor before the big fireplace. She rose, smiling, when Liam introduced himself. "I should have guessed," she said. "But I didn't. Welcome to Carnaby House."

"Nobody warned me, either." Liam's grim mouth moved in a faint grin. "And I didn't realize you were here. I'm afraid I frightened your cousin. Though I didn't mean to."

"You frightened Megan?" Celia asked. "But good heavens, Megan, you are a *mess.* What have you been doing? And you're only wearing one sapphire."

"It was the fog," Megan said quickly. "I couldn't see very well, and I wasn't expecting anyone to be here." But she wondered how Liam had known she was Celia Parr's cousin. Why not just a friend? Why not a married sister? Why not practically anything?

"But your earring," Kristine said. "Mother's earring."

"I'll find it for you, Megan," Liam cut in.

"It doesn't matter. Truly, it doesn't."

Kristine cried, "We have some champagne."

Celia laughed. "My perfect hostess. You must join us, Liam. We'll celebrate your arrival and our return." She looked at Kristine, "Sweetie, run down and get Terrence, will you? He's in the game room, I imagine."

"You're staying aren't you?" Kristine demanded, and at Liam's nod, dashed out.

He bent his dark head and glanced sideways at Megan.

She caught her breath. The sense of familiarity sharpened. She was certain she had known him, somewhere at some time. But in the next instant it was gone.

Celia curled on the floor again, her blue eyes shining, her voice sweet and husky as she talked to Liam, who had taken one of the big leather chairs.

Megan realized suddenly that she had once before seen Celia that way — with Rory when she arranged for them to meet. It was Celia's sign of approval, her response to any attractive man.

Megan glanced at Liam and discovered that

he was looking straight at her, his dark eyes speculative, a frown between his brows.

Terrence came in with Kristine.

"You all right?" he asked Megan before turning to Liam.

She nodded, and Terrence said then, "Did you find everything ready for you, Mr. Judge?"

"Fine, thanks."

"And how long do you plan to stay on?" Terrence asked.

"I haven't decided yet." Liam's eyes once more turned a quick, speculative look on Megan.

She caught it and moved uneasily, wondering who he was, what he was doing in Carnaby House. But the others didn't seem to be concerned.

Terrence poured the champagne, and while Celia passed the glasses around, moving with her peculiar lithe grace, the two men talked of the fog that had settled so stubbornly on the area, and of the Johnstones, their socialite friends, who had put Liam in touch with the Parrs.

Kristine, no longer sullen, sat in her usual place beside Megan, her amber eyes fastened on Liam's suntanned face.

Kristine's change of mood was an accomplishment of Liam's, Megan thought, with sudden wry amusement. But she wished he hadn't come.

At a pause in the conversation, Liam turned to her. "Am I forgiven?"

She heard the teasing undertone in his voice and said coldly, "Yes."

"But you never said what happened," Kristine cried.

"Nothing," Megan said.

Liam suddenly grinned.

The fleeting impression of familiarity rose and quickly faded.

"It didn't seem like nothing at the time, did it?"

Megan, at Kristine's insistence, explained briefly, playing down her fear as much as she could.

"But who on earth did you think he was?" Celia cried.

Terrence laughed. "You always were full of fancies, weren't you, Megan?"

"Fancies?" Liam repeated softly.

Megan didn't answer him.

There was a small cold silence.

She felt Celia and Terrence staring at her.

But then Terrence grinned. He went to her, refilled her half-empty glass. "Drink up, darling. It's good for you, you know."

There was an odd warmth in his voice. Megan glanced up at him, and he smiled.

"Kristine," Celia said, "be a sweetie, and ask Budgie to dig out some coffee and pie now, will you?"

Megan watched as Kristine hurried out. Her tall slender body swayed, and her shining hair rippled on her shoulders. Her wide pink skirt danced around her. When she came back she had put on more lipstick and freshly powdered her nose.

Megan laughed to herself for the first time in weeks. Kristine was at last showing signs of noticing someone other than Megan. It gave her an odd pang. She wondered if that was what a mother felt see her daughter begin to grow up.

Liam didn't seem to notice, nor did he notice Kristine's shining gaze turn sullen when Celia took her place on the sofa, leaning across Megan and engaged him in conversation.

Budgie brought the coffee and pie. Celia hurried to serve, smiling prettily at Liam.

Kristine immediately sat on the sofa, her eyes bright again.

"What do you do, Liam?" Terrence asked.

"Not much of anything right now, I'm afraid," Liam said easily. "I'm just back from Viet Nam. Taking a short rest."

"That must have been rough," Terrence said.

"It can be rougher at home," Liam told him.

"You make us civilians feel better," Celia laughed.

But Liam, his mouth grim, said, "I didn't mean to."

"You'll find it quiet here," Terrence said after a moment, "maybe too quiet for you. There's only Stoneleigh Village."

"We'll have to show you Stoneleigh," Celia said enthusiastically. "It's a sweet little town and . . ."

"And there's Satan's Pillars, and Satan's Puddle," Kristine put in. "I'll show them to you."

"Satan's Pillars? Satan's Puddle?" Liam repeated.

"The stone piles on the road below," Kristine explained. "And our lake, of course. I'm the only one to guide you there. Celia's not athletic. And Terrence is just plain lazy. Megan used to climb the pillars, but that was a long time ago. She won't do it any more. And the lake . . ."

"I had a look at the lake tonight."

Megan felt herself shrinking, snaillike within herself. She wanted to be away out of that room, anywhere at all, except where she was at that moment. She cried out.

But Liam asked quickly, "What's wrong?"

Celia said in a soft voice, "Megan recently lost a loved one."

"I'm sorry," Liam answered.

Megan swayed on her feet. The coffee cup danced in its saucer.

Terrence took it from her. "You're tired, aren't you, darling?"

She nodded, peculiarly distressed by the possessive note in his light voice.

Without looking at anyone, she stammered an excuse and left the room.

Chapter 7

The crash of drums became a whisper of brushes that faded slowly. The record ended bringing sweet silence.

Megan sighed. For the better part of the day Kristine had been in her room, darting out only to slip one more LP under the needle, returning to discuss what she should wear for dinner that night.

Megan didn't understand the sudden interest in clothes until Kristine told her that after she had gone up to her room the evening before, Celia had invited Liam, and he had happily accepted.

The sweet silence continued. Megan grinned. Kristine had given up on the records, and turned her attention to preparing for the big event.

Megan smoothed her pink wool dress over her slender hips. Her bronze hair glinted in the rose-colored lamp light. She touched rouge to her cheeks, painted on a bright mouth, and saw her face grow familiar again. The haggard look gone. The weakness wiped away. Her brown eyes had always been too big, too shadowed.

She shrugged and turned away from the mirror.

Kristine was still primping, cried from behind her closed door, "Don't wait for me, Megan."

So Megan went down to the drawing room.

Terrence was there mixing drinks. He cocked a blond brow at her. "You look wonderful tonight."

She thanked him. She took her usual place on the sofa.

"How about one right now?"

"Oh, no, I'll wait for the others, Terrence," she told him.

"Celia invited Liam up from the stables." Terrence laughed. "I guess Kristine told you. Anyhow, there's an amusing competition beginning to develop. Between Celia and Kristine."

"I imagine they're both bored and need some diversion."

"Diversion." Terrence brought Megan the drink she had refused. "Go on," he said, "it'll put a shine in your eyes." He paused. Then saying softly, "A bit of romance, or at least the thought of it would do you good, too, Megan."

She gave him a level look out of her shadowed eyes. "I've had all of that I want."

He sat close beside her. "That's a very

. . . well . . . forgive me, Megan, but a very abnormal attitude for you to take. You're too young to bury yourself in the past. You have to look ahead."

She asked herself, with deep cold bitterness, to what must she look ahead. To bestow, along with her love, the kiss of death on one more man? There had been her father, Bob, then Rory. . . .

Terrence and the others considered her to be sinking in grief. The truth was — and she faced it then — that she was enmeshed in fear. An unnameable fear that had come upon her when she realized that the curse of Carnaby had gone with her out of the house and had destroyed Rory. An unnameable fear that had clung to her with tightening tentacles since she had allowed herself to be persuaded to return. And the night before, Liam Judge, intruding his presence, rising out of the mist as a hunched shadow, big, huge, overpowering, had brought her to the very edge of terror.

Who was he?

What did he want?

Why did he look at her, she asked herself, his dark eyes full of unspoken questions?

Terrence, speaking lightly, broke into her thoughts. "No one can turn his back on the future, Megan."

She answered just as lightly, "No one would really try."

But a cold draft touched her, and she heard the sound of voices in the hallway, Budgie's, then the deep one of Liam.

He was smiling when he came in. He wore a dark tweed jacket and dark trousers. His short-cropped hair was brushed smooth.

Terrence, rising to greet him, looked smaller and thinner by comparison.

"More fog," Liam said, coming to Megan. "I know you told me it wasn't important. But I looked this afternoon, and . . ." He held out his hand. Megan's blue sapphire earring sparkled on his palm.

She stared at it, her eyes suddenly stinging with tears. It had mattered more than she told him. She had thought of the earring her mother had once worn, gone forever — while the wind banged the shutters all through the long night.

"Oh, Liam," she stammered, "thank you so much. I never dreamed I'd see it again. How did you . . . ? When . . . ?"

"I found it this afternoon. More luck than anything else."

Megan reached for it, but as her fingers approached his palm she hesitated, not wanting to touch him.

He seemed to know. He turned his hand,

dropped the earring into the cup of her fingers. She closed her fingers around it and felt with a small sense of shock, his warmth in the platinum and in the shining stone.

She was impelled to look up at him.

His dark eyes were slanted to hers that were still full of question.

Celia, in floating red chiffon, broke the silence that had gone on too long. Moments later Kristine came down.

A party atmosphere grew with innumerable drinks before dinner. And then Budgie and Clyde out-did themselves with elaborate service and food.

Celia shone with a special brightness, and Kristine, her amber eyes on Liam, tried to divert him.

But Megan was always aware of his dark slanted glances meeting hers, then shifting away, only to return moments later. She was too aware of his obvious attempts to draw her into the conversation.

She froze into watchful silence, afraid of him, afraid of his interest in her.

Afterwards, in the drawing room, having served brandy in huge shining goblets, Terrence sat down beside her. "You're very quiet, Megan."

"Haven't I always been?" she asked, smiling. But she thought of Vivian, gimlet gray eyes, scented silk, florid face, a picture of disapproval.

"Quiet as a shadow," Terrence agreed.

But Megan thought that the shadow had been the old evil she sensed in Carnaby House, and she had been quiet in order to listen for its footsteps behind her.

Celia cried, "Let's go down to the game room. We'll set some music going and dance."

"Oh, yes," Kristine agreed. "You *do* dance, don't you, Liam?"

"Not well," he told her, his eyes going to Megan.

Terrence took her hand. "I see the expression on your face, darling. You're not leaving us now."

So she went with the others.

Celia put a record on, saying sweetly, "I hope you like to waltz, Liam," and held out her arms.

They made a beautiful couple, she in red chiffon that drifted around her slim body, he straight and dark and lithe.

He danced with Celia and then with Kristine, while Megan dutifully moved within the circle of Terrence's arms.

But when Liam came to her, she stammered, "No, no, thanks. I've had enough."

Somehow he was holding her, and she

moved with him, engulfed in a peculiar joy. Time seemed to draw out, extend as the rhythm of the music claimed her, the strength of his arms enfolded her. She caught a glimpse of Kristine and Celia watching. But Liam held her and moved her on. She forgot the others, even forgot herself, in a brief strange magic.

But the moment ended as the needle squealed on the record and Kristine cried, "Why don't we play pool now? You do like pool, don't you, Liam?"

"Yes. I like pool," he told her, his grim mouth relaxing into a smile. "But I've just discovered that I like dancing more than I thought I did."

Megan stepped away from him, the magic dying swiftly, freeing her to feel the quick spasms of fright that rippled through her.

Terrence took her arm. "The rest of you play. I'm going to put another record on and claim the last dance."

But she refused, and when he joined the others around the table, she slipped away.

She tiptoed past the suit of armor at the mahogany bannister, and climbed the steps slowly, relieved to have escaped from Liam's disturbing presence. But she remembered that as she had gone, his dark head had turned, and his dark eyes had followed her. She knew that she hadn't escaped him for long.

She was right. The next morning he was back.

She sat alone at the breakfast table listening to the whisper of the wind along the balustrades, watching pale fingers of sun creep along the old wallpaper.

She heard Kristine's laughter, and the deeper sound of Liam's voice.

She pushed back her chair.

Budgie said, gray eyes stormy, "Oh no you don't, Megan. You finish your meal."

"I'm not hungry, Budgie. Truly."

"I didn't ask you to be hungry. I intend to put some meat on your bones whether you want me to do it or not. And," she added in her hoarse way, "running away from Liam Judge won't help you. So stop it."

"Running away from Liam?" Megan repeated.

"I said it. Now you listen to me."

Megan didn't have to answer. The door burst open.

"There's sun," Kristine shouted. "Beautiful, beautiful sun."

Megan looked at the window. Yes. The pale fingers of sunlight that had crept along the walls had become lemon-yellow rays at the lace curtain. Sun. The first time since they had come to Carnaby House.

"And look who I brought with me," Kristine went on.

Liam grinned at Megan. "I hope I'm not wearing out my welcome. Kristine insisted."

"Megan gets up early," Kristine said. She patted Liam's arm. "Now you sit down. We'll have something." She turned shining amber eyes on Budgie. "Won't we?"

"You will indeed." Budgie, looking pleased with herself and with Kristine, hurried out.

Kristine went on, "Of course, Celia and Terrence are probably sound asleep."

"Kristine has promised to walk me around Satan's Puddle," Liam said. "Will you come with us?"

"Megan doesn't go there. I told you," Kristine said quickly.

"Oh? Why not?"

"She doesn't like it."

Megan listened, staring into the grounds at the bottom of her coffee cup. No, she thought, I don't walk around Satan's Puddle anymore.

"You do look as if you should see the sun," Liam went on gently. "We could walk somewhere else, Megan."

Kristine made a small impatient sound and flung herself in her chair.

"No," Megan said, "but thank you." She smiled at Kristine. It was time, Megan thought, for her to warn Kristine that a girl who is too obvious about her interest in a man can easily frighten him away.

"So you'll just sit here and think," Liam said softly, his dark eyes slanted at Megan's face.

She didn't answer. She tried to swallow, but her throat was suddenly dry.

Why did he seem so familiar to her? Why did he watch her, his dark eyes full of unasked questions? How had he known she was the Parrs' cousin?

"So you think," he repeated gently.

The comment, full of innuendo, hung between them.

"What do you mean, Liam?" Kristine demanded.

He said, wry amusement touching his mouth, "I'm sure Megan knows."

The lemon-pale sun had faded. White fingers of mist drifted against the window again. The room was suddenly filled with shadows.

Megan got to her feet. "I'll see you later."

Budgie cried, "Wait a minute."

But Megan retreated to her room.

It, too, was full of shadows.

But there, at least, she could look at them and know that Liam Judge was not watching her.

She closed the maroon drapes against the

drifting mists. She turned on all the rose-colored lamps, as if soft light would keep the dangerous dark at bay.

There was a movement. Something. Something shifted across the room.

Her heart began to pound. She turned quickly.

Her slender reflection, white blouse and black skirt confronted her. Her wide brown eyes stared back at her, mirroring expected horrors.

She saw her mouth open wide, heard herself laugh, heard the shrill sound of hysteria. She pressed her hands to her mouth.

She was suddenly in Budgie's arms. She was clasped, shaken and crooned at.

The shrill sound faded, and Budgie pushed her into an easy chair before the fireplace.

Megan hiccuped, and trembled, and finally was still.

Budgie said, "You have to stop it. You have to, Megan."

And Clyde nodded nervously. "We knocked, but you couldn't hear us, Megan."

"I'm sorry," Megan gasped. "I'm okay now. Really."

"But you do have to stop." Budgie's wary gray eyes stared down at her. "Now, tell me, what happened?"

Megan grinned. "Nothing. Really. I guess

I'm afraid of my own shadow."

"But laughing like that?" Clyde asked, the ravines deep in his cheeks.

"It was . . ." Megan chuckled, "no, I'm sorry . . . I saw my reflection in the mirror, and it scared me so . . . and when I realized, well . . ."

"It's the brooding," Clyde said heavily, nodding, nodding again. His black eyes peered from under wrinkled lids. "You always were a broody one, Megan. And this . . . this is dangerous."

Budgie took it up. "You'll make something terrible happen to you, Megan."

"*I'll* make . . ." Megan whispered.

"Yes. Yes," Budgie said hoarsely. "It can happen that way. It can. It can."

"*I'll* make something happen," Megan repeated. "But don't you remember the way it was? Not I, Budgie! Not I!" Her voice shook. She fought for control and somehow found it and went on slowly and calmly, "Don't you remember that day on the steps?"

Budgie whispered, "The curse. You thought of that again, did you?" She shook her head, and her iron-gray braids seemed to loosen. "Megan, Megan, that was just a way of speaking. There's no curse. No curse at all. Except . . . except . . . God save you . . . the one in you. The one in you, Megan."

"In me?" Megan repeated. "The curse in me?"

"And I don't believe it. I don't and won't. But you must be careful."

Clyde's big head nodded. "Megan, did you ever learn why your father brought you and Kristine here to Carnaby House?"

"Mother had died," Megan whispered. "You both know that. You know that my mother had died and . . ."

"But where?" Clyde asked. "How? Why?"

Megan cringed in the big chair, filled with a dread she had never known before. She didn't want to hear the answers. She didn't want to know. But she had to. She waited, breath held.

"In that year after Kristine was born," Budgie said gently, "in that year your mother lost her mind, Megan. She went quite mad, and was put away, and she died there — in that place. She was sick, poor girl — just as your father told you. And when she was gone, he brought you and Kristine here, to your Aunt Vivian's and my care."

"She went quite mad," Megan whispered.

"Vivian had promised your father never to tell you. She kept her word. But she watched you, Megan. She waited. She hoped." Budgie sighed. "She had always hated your mother, who had been a poor girl, a waitress in

Stoneleigh Village, until your father married her. And you were so like her. Small and frail with the same bright hair, the same withdrawal. Yes, Vivian waited and hoped. She thought to control the money your father had left. But you were strong, Megan. You must be strong now."

So that was why Budgie and Clyde watched her with wary eyes. They were afraid, afraid of what could happen to her.

"Are you saying . . ." she subdued the tremor in her voice, "are you saying that I am . . . that I am mad, too?"

Clyde rumbled, "Megan, no! But you must let the past die."

"It has died," she said quietly.

But she thought of the curse of Carnaby. Her father, Bob and Rory. They were all dead. Had she imagined the connection? Had she been mad, quite mad, like her mother since the time she was seventeen? Was she mad to think that evil walked beside her as she moved through Carnaby House?

Budgie touched her cheek. "You'll be all right?"

Megan answered through dry lips, "But don't tell Kristine. Promise me. Don't ever tell Kristine."

Budgie and Clyde promised and left Megan.

Alone, she went to the mirror. She stared

into her eyes. She examined the curve of her cheek, the shape of her mouth. She stepped back and peered through the rose-colored light, wondering if she were looking into the face of madness.

Chapter 8

Two days passed, then three. Time moved slowly while she absorbed the facts of her mother's death, what might be a weakness in herself.

Liam came and went with disturbing frequency, but she avoided him as much as she could.

Kristine trailed him like a puppy that had, without invitation, adopted a new master.

She had stared at Megan when Megan told her, "It takes finesse to win a man, darling. And he must be almost thirty, rather old for you."

"What do you care?" she demanded. "You don't want him, do you?"

Megan caught her breath. "Kristine!"

But Kristine grinned, threw herself into Megan's arms. "You don't know how I feel. I'll always love you most, of course, but Liam . . . oh Megan, Liam makes me know that I'm a woman."

Megan, caught between laughter and tears, said gently, "I don't want you to be hurt, Kristine. We don't really know Liam."

Kristine's eyes were expressionless again.

"Is that all?" she asked.

Celia, more subtle and more adult, made an equally strong bid for Liam's attention.

Yet Megan knew and sensed that though she in no way encouraged him, he came to the big house daily to see her, and that he shamelessly exploited Kristine and Celia to that end.

It was one more reason, Megan told herself, for her to dislike him. More. To fear him.

She knew he had had a reason for renting the stables and coming to Carnaby House. She knew that some time soon, in some way, she would learn what that reason was.

Terrence had begun to show plainly that he resented Liam's almost constant presence and finally said to her, "One of these days, I'm going to tell him we didn't rent our home to him. The agreement was for the stables."

"And why did you?" she asked.

He shrugged. "It was Celia's idea. We needed the money. Why else would we, Megan?"

"I wondered." Megan smiled. "Anyway, Kristine and Celia enjoy having him."

"And what about you?" Terrence asked softly.

"Me?" Megan shrugged. "It doesn't matter to me."

"Doesn't it, Megan? I've seen you look at

him. I've seen the way he looks at you."

But Megan did not dare put into words to Terrence, nor to anyone, her uneasy feeling that Liam's presence was a threat to her.

"I have no interest in him," she said.

Terrence grinned. "That's good. I was beginning to be afraid that he had won all my women from me." Terrence's face sobered. "And if he'd won you, that would have been the worst."

She said uneasily, "Now, Terrence, that's silly."

"Is it? Don't you know how I feel about you?" His self-indulgent mouth tightened. "I'm sure I've made it quite plain."

"You've always been good to me," she said lightly.

"Good to you?" A pale brow arched. "Is that all you've thought?" He paused, then, "Listen, Megan, I wanted to give you more time. But now . . . well . . . I can't wait any more. I wanted you to know, to realize, I've always felt this way about you . . . I . . ."

She said quickly, "Terrence, I do think. . . ."

But he went on, "We could make a good life together. You and me. Think about it, Megan. I know I can make you happy, happier than you've ever been."

His arms came around her. His lips brushed hers.

She was too startled even to draw away.

He raised his head. "You see, darling?"

"We're cousins," she gasped. "Why, Terrence . . ."

He grinned. "Many first cousins marry. It's the common thing among the royal families in Europe, so don't look at me as if I'm suggesting incest."

She moved out of his arms. "I'm not thinking of marriage now, Terrence. Not to anyone."

"Don't say that. Give yourself time to get used to the idea. See if it doesn't grow on you, Megan."

Liam appeared in the doorway behind Terrence.

Megan wondered how long he had been there and what he had heard. She said quickly, "I'll see you later," and went upstairs.

She slept badly that night. She dreamed that the suit of armor in the great hallway below had come to creaking life and found its way to her room, and it was suddenly a man. A man with Liam's face that was tanned and square-jawed. A man with Liam's face who bent over her, his arms reaching while the room echoed with the sound of sweet, wild laughter — and Megan recognized her mother's voice.

She awakened trembling. The room was

cold, still and empty.

Dawn came in pale and misty before she slept again.

Chapter 9

It happened the next evening.

The house was empty. Budgie and Clyde had taken a rare day off and driven away, Megan didn't know where. Terrence and Celia, grown restless, had gone to Stoneleigh Village. They had asked Kristine and Megan to go with them, but Megan refused, and Kristine insisted that she would stay with her sister. By the time early twilight fell, Kristine, too, had become restless and went out for a walk. When she didn't return, Megan decided that she had gone to the stables to visit with Liam.

Megan wandered from room to room, listening to the faint whispers that were part memory of the past and part wind at the balustrades, that seemed to grow louder as the waning light cast thicker shadows in the gloom.

She supposed that there would always be moments when she would remember love and need, but she had put those dreams behind her now. The curse of Carnaby would never hurt anyone again.

Perhaps it was mad to believe it. Perhaps

there was reason for the wary glances that Budgie and Clyde gave her.

But she knew. She knew with an instinct that was part of life itself that something or someone hated her and had judged her undeserving of love when she was a child. This thing had put *the mark* on her for life.

The twilight thickened perceptibly as she went down the steps. The suit of armor seemed to lean towards her as she hurried past it. Faint light touched the bits and bridles, the crossed swords on the wall.

In the drawing room, she lit the fire. She went to the window to draw the heavy green drapes. The twilight, filled with mist, lay like a blanket on the grounds. She saw a faint light from the stables, and sighed, wishing that Kristine would return, then reminding herself that it was good for Kristine to be away from her for a little while.

Still she wondered uneasily, if it were good for Kristine to spend so much time with Liam, who treated her with good-natured, big brother camaraderie, as he watched Megan — a silent question written on his grim face.

The logs in the fireplace settled and sent up a drift of embers.

Megan took a book and settled in her usual place on the sofa. Slowly, the bright flames warmed her. Slowly, the words on the page before her came into focus and began to make sense. Briefly, she found an escape from her thoughts.

Soon a cold draft touched her. She shivered and looked up. There was no sound. No movement. But the flames leaped high in the fireplace.

She watched them, remembering how she had seen her father's face, Bob's and Rory's form in other flames.

She closed her eyes and leaned forward.

She heard a faint sound nearby.

Before she could respond, she was flung forward. She felt an explosion of pain and crumpled, falling into spinning lights as brilliant as stars. Through the pain, she heard a great terrible sound of a huge metal bell. Then it faded and became the whisper of tiptoeing footsteps that receded. Receded, as though she had cried out for help. She heard the whisper of those tiptoeing footsteps through dense waves of blackness. She heard them, and then they were gone.

And she was alone, sinking, sinking. . . .

A weight pressing her down and down harder into the rug. A cool knife cutting into the back of her neck bruising her head. Stunned and only half-conscious, she fought to breathe.

The air was suddenly cold on her cheeks.

A draft touched her hair. Footsteps came closer. Slow ones that suddenly broke into a run.

The weight pinned her. She couldn't move. Terror took her breath.

She heard a deep voice cry, "No, no, Megan."

Liam.

She couldn't scream or struggle.

His big warm hands touched her face and her head.

The weight was suddenly gone, the cool knife-edge of metal withdrawn from her neck.

She opened her eyes.

He was kneeling beside her, his face turned away, his wide shoulders braced as he shifted the heavy copper tray. It tilted, fell and struck an edge of the teak table. The wood splintered and Liam swore. The tray lay where it fell. He turned back to Megan.

"Please," she whispered. "Please . . ." her eyes wide with fear.

"Don't look at me like that. Don't, Megan. I'm not going to hurt you."

With a hard-set expression, he bent over her. His hands touched her swiftly, lightly.

Bewildered, she watched his face. She saw relief come slowly to ease the grimness. She saw the beginnings of a smile.

"Don't move, Megan, not yet," he ordered.

"I want to be sure . . ."

There were more gentle and crooning words, but she didn't listen.

Instead, she heard sounds in her mind — tiptoeing sounds, coming and then receding.

She felt a draft on her face, and heard the quick soft sounds, and felt the blow that had sent her to the floor, and heard, spinning into half-consciousness, the quick soft sounds receding.

"Now," Liam said. "Now, can you tell me what happened?"

"I don't know. I don't know." She tried to think, but pain throbbed through her, echoing the beat of her heart.

"Don't move yet. Wait."

She knew when Liam left her. She knew when he returned.

He said, "I'm going to put a cold towel on your neck. Megan, can you hear me?"

She tried to nod and cried out.

"I said don't move!"

She felt him beside her with his light touch. The cold at first was terrible, then good, bracing.

Liam said, "I'm going to turn you now. Can you hold on to the towel?"

She had learned not to nod. She made a sound of assent and got an arm up. She found his hand and the towel beneath it. She snatched her fingers from his. He caught them and guided them back.

"Hold on," he said, with sudden amusement.

Her head was clearing. The pain ebbed to a dull throb.

"I can get up," she told him.

"Be still."

She felt like a child being lifted and carried to the sofa. There were cushions around her and under her. A cushion braced her head. When he released her, she suddenly felt cold, unprotected. She shivered.

He took off his windbreaker and put it over her and he sat beside her.

She had felt unprotected when he took his arms away from her. Now she suddenly felt threatened by his nearness. She wondered briefly if she *were* mad. She stared up at him feeling confused and frightened.

He said, "Before I call Stoneleigh Village for a doctor, I want to know what happened here."

"You can see," she whispered. "The tray . . . it came away from the wall. And I was sitting there . . ." Her voice trailed off. She remembered the draft and the tiptoeing footsteps. But she couldn't tell him about that. She was afraid. She didn't know him, nor what he wanted from her. She didn't trust him.

"I see the tray. But what happened? Why did it fall?"

"Why did it fall?"

He asked gently, "Megan, are you still afraid of me?"

"No." It was not a convincing lie, she knew at once.

Liam smiled. "Yes, you are. In a way." He shook his head. "But never mind that for now. What else are you afraid of, who else?"

"I?" She managed to make her voice steady. *"I?"*

"You."

"Stop badgering me. My head aches. My neck feels broken. I . . ."

"You're recovering," he said dryly, smiling again.

It was true. The pain still throbbed through her, but she could think. She wondered why Liam had asked her why she was afraid. What did he know? What did he suspect?

"I'd better see about the doctor then."

"It isn't necessary, Liam."

"I think so."

"I'd rather not," she said.

"Megan, do you always argue?"

"I never argue."

He grinned.

She smiled unwillingly. It was a strange conversation, she thought. "But never mind. No doctor."

"We'll see. You're alone in the house, aren't you?"

"Celia and Terrence went into Stoneleigh Village."

"Yes. They asked if I wanted to go. I didn't."

"Then why did you just ask. . . ."

"To be certain. I saw Kristine a while ago, wandering outside in the gardens. And Budgie and Clyde left in the afternoon." He added slowly, "I thought Kristine might have come back."

"Not yet." Megan stared at him. "You *knew* I was alone, didn't you?"

"I wasn't sure. I told you. I thought Kristine might have come back. But I took a chance and came up to the door, and . . ."

She looked at him with doubt in her eyes.

"Why should I want to hurt you?" he demanded.

She didn't know. She couldn't explain what she felt, not to herself, not to him.

"Why should anyone want to hurt you, Megan? Can you tell me that?"

"It was an accident," she said. "It must have been."

"That thing has been standing there for . . . well, how long?" He waited, but she didn't answer. "For years of course. Years, Megan. Well, what about it?"

She didn't say anything.

He sighed. "Why are you so frightened?"

"I?"

"You." His voice became very gentle. "I've known that since I first saw you."

She closed her eyes lest he read her thoughts in them. She had seen the second face of the evil in Carnaby House. She knew what he didn't know. Someone had been in the hallway and standing near the door when she sat in her usual place on the sofa under the huge tray. Someone had seen the tray fall, heard her cry out and disappeared.

"Has it something to do with Rory?" Liam asked. "Couldn't you try to trust me just a little? Couldn't you tell me that much?"

"With Rory?" she cried. "What do you know about Rory?"

"That you were engaged to him." Liam's voice became hard and very deep as he went on. "He committed suicide two days before you were to be married."

"How do you know all of that about me?"

"Kristine," he said quickly.

"Kristine." It could have been true, Megan thought. Yet she didn't believe him. He had answered too swiftly, as if he had practiced it, preparing himself for when she asked that question. "Who are you, Liam, what do you want?"

"I'll tell you all that later, Megan."

"Later? Perhaps later will be *too* late."

He leaned closer to her. "Listen, don't you see? That's why I'm asking. Is it the house you fear? Can it be that?" When she didn't answer, he went on thoughtfully, "I feel something. Something I don't understand. I feel . . ."

"It isn't your business," she told him.

"Isn't it?"

"You said you came up to the door, Liam. You thought I was alone. You wanted to see me. Why?"

"To ask you the questions that I've been asking." He smiled, but the grim look remained around his mouth. "I hope you don't mind that I just walked in when I saw the door open. I heard the crash and came to investigate."

"I appreciate your interest and concern, believe me."

"I don't think you do. I think you wish I were miles away from this place and you."

She asked suddenly, "Could we have met before? Is it possible that I knew you somewhere at some time?"

"I don't see how, Megan."

"But there are moments, I know it seems

. . ." she had been going to say 'mad' . . . but suddenly she couldn't use that word. "I mean, I know it seems odd, but I have the feeling just once in a while that . . ."

"I'd remember," he said gravely. "I know I'd remember, Megan."

"A long time ago? Perhaps some relative of yours, Liam, that looks like you?"

"That's hardly possible, is it?" Liam paused. "Megan, are you sure that your feeling has nothing to do with Rory's death?"

She stared at Liam and shook her head slowly.

"Then what about Bob?"

She gasped, "Bob? Why do you ask about him now? How do you know about him, too?"

"Kristine told me, of course. She said that's why you were so upset when you saw me near Satan's Puddle. She said you have a thing about Bob. And always have had. And a thing about Rory now, too."

Megan said coldly, "I'll have to tell Kristine not to discuss my personal affairs with strangers."

"I'm not exactly a stranger. Not any more. At least I don't want to be."

She moved her legs and threw aside his windbreaker. "I'll get up now."

"Wait," he said.

But when she moved again, he shifted back. As she got her feet to the floor and got her head up, pain throbbed through her. She pressed her hands to her bronze curls, waiting until dizzying waves subsided.

Liam put a hand on her knee. "Is it bad?"

"No. Just for a minute . . ."

"Megan, listen, I have a reason for asking you these questions." He went on, as if reassured, but his eyes watched her.

"What reason?"

He hesitated. "I think you should answer."

"But *you* haven't answered *me,* Liam."

"I know. I know." He waited. Then he took a deep audible breath. "Megan, when Bob died . . . no, don't flinch so . . . just try to think and remember. Did you wonder how it happened?"

Had she wondered? She didn't know. It was the curse — the curse. But she couldn't tell Liam that. She said what they had all said, "It was an accident, Liam." The words sounded too familiar. She knew that she had said the same thing about the way the giant copper tray had come down from the wall not long before. "An accident," she repeated, to drown out that thought.

"Yes. All right, Megan. But why? Why?" He paused, "Why then in particular?"

But she couldn't listen to him any longer.

She forced herself to her feet. "Thanks for your help, Liam. I appreciate it." She tried to keep her voice steady. She strove to keep her steps steady. She moved carefully, feeling as if the rug were too far from her feet. Her head ached. Her neck was stiff.

A breath behind her, Liam said, "Just a minute, Megan."

But she didn't stop to answer him. She didn't want him to know her terror. She was at the door. He took her arm. "I'll walk you up to your room." Her voice was polite. "No. It's not necessary, thank you."

He ignored that, and she didn't dare stop to argue with him. She went on out into the hallway past the suit of armor that leaned at the staircase. She climbed the broad, carpeted stairs cautiously, moving forward into the pink glow of the upper hall. She moved slowly as he went with her. Between them, moving slowly, came fear.

"You're shivering," he said.

"Please, Liam, please," she answered, "just go away."

Chapter 10

He stood in the center of her room studying it from narrowed eyes. "A perfect place for a nightmare," he said finally. "Why do you put up with it?"

"Please," she said, "just go away."

"Again?" He slanted a look at her and then went to turn on the rose-colored lamps. "That's better. But not much."

She sank into the easy chair before the hearth.

"What about a fire, Megan?"

She shook her head, but he took out matches; and in moments, the flames leaped up and caught. He straightened up and grinningly said, "Clyde knows how to lay the logs, doesn't he?"

She didn't answer.

"Now," Liam said, "about Bob, Megan."

Her head gave a great throb of pain. She winced, shivered. "I can't think about it now."

But Liam stood over her, staring into her eyes.

She remembered the peculiar joy she had felt in his arms. She shivered again.

He said, "You have to think about it some

time, don't you? You have to think about Bob and about Rory."

She shook her head again.

"You'll just go on being afraid. Until . . . until what, Megan?"

She thought of the sunlit day Bob died. They had made plans to elope that night.

"Answer me," Liam insisted, his voice hard. As hard as his dark eyes, his grim mouth.

She knew he had said the same thing more than once, perhaps twice.

She whispered, "What do you want? Who are you, Liam?"

"A friend to you. That should be enough."

"A friend to me?" She found, surprisingly, that she could smile bitterly. "You?"

"You don't believe that, do you?"

"No. No. I can't."

"It's just as well. Perhaps you should trust no one. No one at all, Megan."

"But you," she insisted. "Why should you care? About Bob and Rory? And why now?"

"I have my own reasons. And since you don't trust me, I see no purpose in explaining to you," he said.

"You owe me that much, Liam."

"Perhaps I do," he said thoughtfully. "I'm a friend of the Johnstones, who put me in touch with the Parrs when they heard that I wanted a place out in this area."

"And why here?"

"It's pleasant." There was sudden laughter in his voice. "I'm recuperating, I told you. Viet Nam, if you recall."

"Recuperating from what, though?" she demanded.

"Fatigue." He grinned. "The kind that doesn't show, but it turned out to be more isolated than I thought. So when I met you, and the others, well, I was delighted. Let's just say I got interested. I'm that kind of man. I get interested in . . . in things. And that's it." He came and stood over her, hands in his pockets, wide shoulders hunched.

She tried not to but she shrank back.

"You *are* afraid of me," he said, then added thoughtfully, "Perhaps you want to be. It's easier that way."

"I'm tired, Liam."

"Or is it my questions that scare you so?"

"I'm tired," she repeated.

"Yes. I guess you are. Fear *is* tiring, isn't it?"

She didn't answer that.

He sighed. "Megan, about Rory . . . how could he have done it? Why? Why would a man like Rory Ford . . . ?"

Her wide brown eyes narrowed as she glanced at Liam. "Did you know Rory?"

Liam said, "I feel as if I did, but that isn't

telling me what I asked."

She cried, "Don't you think I've asked myself the same question a thousand times? Don't you think I want to know? Rory? It's unbelievable. He was always so happy, so easy. And he didn't have to do it. No matter what . . ."

"Yes? No matter what . . . ?"

"No matter what happened, I would have . . . I would have understood. I . . . even if . . . oh, I see it now. But I didn't know then. Truly, I didn't!"

"Wait, Megan. What do you mean?"

She heard the sharp note in Liam's voice. She shrank into the easy chair, and turned away from his compelling gaze to stare into the fire. She wouldn't say the words aloud. But they echoed in her mind bitter as acid. She had not loved Rory. She had needed him as a child needs a parent. She had needed his laughter. Even if he had sensed the emptiness of her childish bond, he could have freed himself. He *didn't* have to die.

She bent her head. Tears stung her eyes.

Liam said, "Don't, Megan. Please, be careful, will you?"

She didn't acknowledge the light touch of his hand on her hair. It was quickly withdrawn.

In a moment, the door closed.

She was alone.

The room was still.

The fire burned low with its warmth fading.

Liam had said, 'Be careful.' And he didn't know about the small sounds in the hallway, the cold draft on her face.

Liam had asked about Rory, and about Bob. And he didn't know about the curse that was upon her in Carnaby or outside it.

It seemed a long time before she moved. She pushed herself out of the deep chair, giddy with a sudden throb in her head. She opened the door, and listened. The house was still empty. But she heard, with an unnamed sense, the whisper of an old evil wandering in the dark.

She had to know.

She went softly along the long hall. She crept down the stairs. The suit of armor, lance pointed at her heart, waited there. She circled it warily to peer into the drawing room.

Everything was the same as when she and Liam had left it.

The copper tray lay where Liam put it when he shifted its murderous weight from her crumpled body. The smashed teak table was on its side near the sofa.

There was a pale, faded place on the wall above the spot where Megan usually sat, a huge faded place that showed where the tray had hung for so many years.

She had been looking into the flames, remembering that she had seen the faces of her loved ones there. She had bent forward. So the falling tray struck her a glancing blow.

She forced herself to go into the drawing room.

She crouched over the tray, slowly and cautiously ran her fingers around its heavily-carved rim. The metal was cool yet seemed to burn her flesh. There were several places that seemed sticky. She bent close to examine them and found thin edges of torn tape. Clinging to them were shredded strands of strong black thread.

Wide-eyed, she looked up. There had been a faint sound from somewhere outside. She waited and listened. But nothing happened.

Trembling, she rose. She backed away from the copper tray, the old and familiar thing that had been used as a weapon against her.

She knew. She was certain.

She supposed that she could have imagined the tiptoe sounds, but the edges of tape, the black thread that seemed to burn her fingertips. She hadn't imagined *them.*

She pictured it. Someone, a shadowy form, climbed on a chair that morning or the morning before? Quick hands set tape and thread. In a few moments, it was done and the chair replaced. The black thread concealed along the floorboards and drawn out into the hall. Someone, a shadowy form, waiting. As Megan studied the flames, someone came in through the front door, tiptoed down the hall, knelt in the dark to pull the black threads, and then when the tray came down, tiptoed away again.

Someone had tried to kill her.

But who? Who hated her? Who wanted to see her dead? Who wore a smiling mask to cover the frowning face of evil?

They were all family. Celia. Terrence. Kristine. And Budgie and Clyde were as good as family. Each of them known since childhood. Each of them trusted. How could Megan suspect them now?

She pressed her hands to her throbbing head.

Or, doubt flickered through her, was there some justice in Budgie's wary glances, in Clyde's rumbled warnings?

Briefly, Megan wondered if she had brooded herself into that same madness that had been her mother's ruin.

But, though it might be easier to accept madness than the meaning of the attack on her, Megan shrugged that doubt aside. She was not mad. The falling tray had been intended to destroy her.

But who?

She looked slowly around the room, staring

at its familiar furnishings as though they could tell her who her enemy was.

Liam's windbreaker lay on the sofa where she had left it.

She went to it, hesitantly picked it up, remembering how he had draped it around her, the peculiar joy she felt at his touch, the joy that drowned in quick hot fear.

Liam.

He was in and out of Carnaby House. He could have tampered with the tray and set the threads. He had been lurking nearby and knew she was alone. He could have struck at her from the hallway, and then come in to see if his work had been well done, and, finding her alive, he could have pretended at shock.

But why?

And why had he come to Carnaby House?

Why did he ask about Bob? About Rory?

She had to know, to understand. She would ask him. She would look into his dark somber eyes, and ask him, and she would see, recognize, the truth.

She didn't stop to think. Holding the windbreaker against her, she hurried outside.

It was cold, dark. Through the bare trees, she saw a light in the stables window. She hesitated, shivering, on the wide stone steps. Then she ran down the slope.

She paused in front of the door. Through its glass pane, she could see him. He sat at a table, head bent on folded arms, his wide shoulders sagging.

Her throat tightened. A small cold finger of fear ran down her spine.

She decided to leave the windbreaker on the stoop and return to the house. She decided that she didn't want to question him after all.

But, as she backed away, he glanced up.

He got to his feet, crossed the room, and had the door open before she had gone two steps.

"Megan!"

She turned slowly, shivering, to face him.

"What is it?"

She held out the windbreaker. "I brought you this."

He came to her and took it from her hands. "Come in."

She followed him meekly.

Inside, with the door closed, her escape sealed, he said, "All right. You brought me this." He flung the jacket on a chair. "And . . ."

He loomed over her, close, threatening, head bent, dark eyes fixed on her face.

"Liam," she asked. "Liam, was it you?"

She had thought, she had been certain, that she would see the truth, know it when she heard it, recognize that reply more clearly than any other.

But when he answered her, his voice grim, his dark somber eyes meeting hers without a flicker, she was more confused than ever.

"No," he said gravely. "You have nothing to fear from me any longer, Megan. But there is someone. . . ." His hands that were warm and strong cupped her cheeks. "There is someone, Megan. And now that you admit it to me, to yourself . . ."

She pulled away from him. The instinct that was stronger than life itself warned her of danger.

"No, Liam," she cried, backing to the door.

He said, "Megan, wait."

But she left him. She ran up the slope to the house.

Chapter 11

The drums awakened her. She lay still, allowing the faint throb of pain to possess her and occupy her total consciousness. But it soon faded. She sat up, looking into the circles of rose-colored light on the rug, and wondered what the day would bring. One attack had failed. Would there be another?

The drum roll ended with impressive flourishes.

There was sweet silence for a few moments. Megan wondered why Kristine had such fondness for that particular record. Then the door smashed open.

Kristine was there, crying, "Megan? Are you up? How does your head feel?"

"I'm up, and it's okay."

"Isn't it crazy, the way that big tray fell down off the wall? Clyde said it couldn't have happened in a million years. But it did. And the table broken to bits, too. Clyde's getting it back up now, rumbling and grumbling about it, too." Still talking, Kristine opened the maroon drapes and peered out. "Misty. Black clouds in the east." She swung around to look at Megan. "Are you sure you're okay?"

"Of course I'm sure." Megan knew her smile wasn't much but it was the best she could do. "Accidents like that happen sometimes."

"You were lucky." Kristine's wide amber eyes shone. "Clyde said if it had really hit you straight on . . ."

"Well, it didn't."

"Clyde said that Liam was here with you, when . . ."

"He was at the door about to knock. He heard the crash and came in."

"I should have been with you. But I went for a walk, and I was hoping I'd see him."

"He knew you were in the gardens for a while. He told me so."

Kristine peered at Megan through the veil of her shining hair. "Honestly, how come I missed him anyhow? But then I went down to the lake, and was wishing I'd gone with Celia and Terrence to Stoneleigh Village."

"Are they up yet?" Megan, at the closet, chose a red blouse and skirt. "They were late coming in."

"No." Kristine sighed. "I hope today is better than yesterday. Between your accident, and me with nothing to do . . ." She sighed again. "I hope I see Liam anyhow."

Megan dressed, brushed her hair, made up her face.

Her big brown eyes seemed larger than ever, feverishly bright.

Kristine, watching, said suddenly, "You don't like Terrence, do you?"

"Of course I do," Megan answered. "We're cousins, family. I think it's childish of you to say such a thing."

"Maybe it is. But Terrence said it first," Kristine shrugged.

Megan turned to look at her. "What do you mean?"

"I heard him tell Celia that he was afraid there wasn't much chance for him. Not as long as Liam hung around. And couldn't she think of some way to dislodge him."

Megan said thoughtfully, "That was a childish thing for Terrence to say."

"Was it?" Kristine demanded. "You do like Liam best."

Megan's heart gave a queer little flutter, but she answered steadily, "I don't like anyone best." She went on, "And now that we're on the subject, I want to ask a favor of you." She hesitated and then went on. "I gather that Liam has been asking you questions about me, Kristine. And I don't like that, nor do I like the idea that you might discuss me or my personal affairs with a stranger."

"Liam isn't a stranger," Kristine said coldly. But then she grinned, her small red mouth softening. "Besides, he didn't ask questions. I told him about Bob. Because of that night that you were so silly about seeing him on the bluffs. And Celia said you were bereaved, so I had to explain about Rory."

"I see. But just the same . . ."

"What difference does it make?"

"Perhaps none."

"Well, then. . . ." Kristine went to the door, clutching her pink robe around her. "I'll get dressed, too. See you in a minute."

Megan nodded. "I'll be downstairs."

As she went to the dining room, she wondered what the words Terrence had said to Celia actually meant. Kristine had taken them to indicate jealousy of Liam. But Megan saw another explanation. Was Terrence the one wearing a mask to cover his true face, who had attempted to kill her? Did Terrence mean that Liam's presence was a hindrance? And why? Why?

She had wondered at the sudden romantic interest Terrence had shown in her. She had rejected his proposal.

She stopped at the door of the dining room.

Celia and Terrence were not just talking poor. They had run through the money left them.

Money.

Could Terrence have asked her to marry

him for that, and being rejected, had he decided that with her dead, and he and Celia joint executors of the estate Kristine would inherit, they could recoup the fortune they had thrown away?

Megan shivered, reached for the door, then paused again.

"But does she know?" Budgie was asking.

"I can't tell," Clyde rumbled. "Just watch her. What else is there to do?"

Megan's cold fingers trembled as she opened the door and went in.

Budgie smiled anxiously, "Feel better today? Your neck all right, Megan?"

Megan, nodding, sat at the table.

"I'll get you your coffee," Clyde rumbled, the ravines deep in his gaunt cheeks. He went out.

Budgie was beginning to say something, Megan never knew what, when there was a knock at the front door. With another anxious look at Megan, Budgie went to answer it. She returned with Liam.

He stood in the doorway, and said quickly, "I won't stay. I just stopped by to see how you are, Megan."

"I'm recovered," she told him.

He hesitated, looked at Budgie, looked at Clyde who had returned with a coffeepot. "Well, I'll be around," he told Megan finally.

"I mean . . . if you want me for anything."

She thanked him, and after another hesitation, he nodded and left.

Relieved that he had gone, Megan sipped the coffee Clyde had poured for her, and watched the thickening fingers of mist drift by the window.

Moments later, Kristine hurried in. "I thought I saw Liam on the slope."

"He was here for a minute," Budgie told her.

"He was!" she wailed. "And I missed him?" She turned to Megan, demanded, "Did you invite him for dinner?"

Megan shook her head.

"But why not? Honestly, Megan . . ."

"I didn't think of it, Kristine."

"Celia would have," Kristine said sulkily.

"Celia would have what?" She was in the doorway, her triangular face full of curiosity. She wore a black shirt, black trousers and a heavy silver belt.

"You'd have asked Liam to dinner," Kristine told her.

"That I would." Celia's smile glowed as she joined Megan at the table. "And don't worry, sweetie, I shall. I'll call him a little later."

"I'd better go see what I'm going to wear," Kristine cried, and hurried out.

Celia winked at Megan. "That's a fair-sized crush she has."

"I'm afraid so," Megan agreed. She went on, trying to be casual, "By the way, Celia, speaking of Liam indirectly, I was wondering how it happened that you rented the stables out."

"How it happened?" Celia repeated. "We needed the money. Why else?"

"And Liam was recommended by the Johnstones?"

"Oh yes, I told you. Eva had heard me say the stables were available, and she probably heard me bemoan the scarcity of renters around here. So, when she ran into Liam, she put him in touch with me."

"Do you suppose she knew we were coming up here?"

"I expect so. I had told her we were going to try to talk you into it anyway." Celia grinned. "But of course, I never dreamed you'd get hit on the head by a tray, Megan. Now, really, that was . . ."

Megan ignored that. She said, "Liam told us that he didn't know anyone was in Carnaby House, Celia."

Celia's blond brows arched. "What of it? Eva needn't have told him, you know. She probably wouldn't have thought it any of his business particularly."

"And you never saw him before he came to the house?"

"Of course not! We arranged it all by phone." She grinned. "And I admit I didn't guess what an attractive man I was talking to."

"Did you get references?"

Celia stared at her, looked at Budgie, shrugged, and once more stared at Megan. "What are you getting at? Yes. We got references. The Johnstones." Her pale blue eyes narrowed. "Megan, really, you do sound *so* peculiar."

"We don't know anything about him," Megan said. "Why he's here . . . why he . . ."

"He's recuperating from Viet Nam. Remember? That's all we need to know, isn't it? That and he's good company, pleasant to look at and interesting." Celia put her coffee cup down. "And now, if you'll excuse me, Megan, I'll go and invite him for dinner."

Kristine, hands on her hips, stood in the doorway. "When a girl is in love," she said bitterly, "she wants to know everything, everything, about her sweetheart. That's why Megan keeps asking questions about Liam."

Megan gasped, "Kristine!"

Celia laughed.

Kristine grinned suddenly. "Megan, you should see your face! You look positively outraged. And just because I teased you." She spun on her toes. "I decided on this. What do you think?"

She was wearing pale green chiffon, that was low in front and back and snug at her tiny waist. Her hair was drawn into a ponytail and bound with a ribbon that matched her gown.

"You look lovely," Megan told her.

"And you'll get it all messed up before dinnertime," Budgie said.

Celia grinned. "I better get a move on. The competition is fierce around here, you know."

Kristine giggled, but her wide amber eyes were absolutely blank.

Clyde paused beside Megan to fill her wine glass. Candlelight danced on his gaunt face. His eyes, black as coal chips, slanted down to her in a quick look. Then he moved on to serve Kristine.

Megan looked around the table at the others.

Terrence caught her eye and grinned. "Good thing you've got such a hard head. And you know what I mean, too."

It was easier to pretend she didn't know that he was referring, not to the blow she had gotten the day before, but to his second proposal made and refused that afternoon.

She sipped her wine, wondering how she could sit so quietly and calmly, while with her sat someone who wanted to kill her. Her family. A single stranger.

She put her glass down carefully. Her eyes moved to Celia, whose piled-high blonde hair gleamed in the light. She was turned, smiling at Liam, smiling in sweet approval. Celia, Megan knew, was more than casually interested in the tall, sunburned man with dark somber eyes. Celia wanted him for herself. And she, like Terrence, had expensive tastes. Perhaps Megan's money was another thing Celia wanted.

And Kristine, sweet Kristine, Megan thought, once so loving, possessive, now, suddenly aware of, attracted to, Liam. With Megan dead, Kristine would have the freedom of an adult. She . . . But Megan couldn't bear the things in her mind.

Budgie, at the sideboard, Clyde next to her, had been Megan's allies in the old days when Vivian, in scented silk, turned every hour cold. But, with Megan dead, Celia and Terrence in control of Kristine's wealth, Budgie and Clyde would no longer be confined to two rooms except for those few times a year when Carnaby House was opened.

Megan slid a glance at Liam, and found that his dark look was slanted at her. He didn't seem disturbed that she had caught him watching her again.

His eyes met hers.

It was an odd look, frightening.

Then he turned his head.

She saw briefly that odd familiarity that had troubled her ever since the first time she had seen him. Since the night he had been a hunched shadow in the mist, then a pursuer, calling, "Wait. Don't be afraid."

She set her wine glass down carefully.

Who was he? What did he want?

Chapter 12

She had left the others and gone to her room.

Now, though it was late, music and laughter filtered up the stairs along the tunnel of the hallway.

She sat in the easy chair, and stared into the fire, thinking. Someone wanted to kill her. Someone. Soon. In Carnaby House. She could trust no one. No one at all.

She had thought several times during the day that she would pack, slip down the steps, find the keys to the car, and disappear forever.

But she knew that could not save her. She could not escape her fate. She mustn't try. She had to wait, to wait in Carnaby House, for either life, or death.

There was a gentle tap at the door. She turned her head slowly. "Yes!"

Clyde said, "Megan? Something for you."

"Come on in."

He had a pot of coffee on a silver tray, a Meissen cup, a single bronze chrysanthemum. "All settled for the night, Megan?"

She nodded, aware of the worried look in his coal chip eyes.

"Budgie thought you might want something

warm," Clyde grinned, pointing at the flower. "And Terrence sent this along. He said it would match your hair."

"Tell him I said 'thanks,' will you?" she remarked dryly.

The ravine in Clyde's right cheek became a dimple. "What? You don't like the message?"

"Oh, Terrence . . ." she shrugged. "You know him."

"Some girl could do worse, Megan."

"*Some* girl," she agreed. "But not me."

Clyde nodded, nodded nervously. "Rest well, Megan."

She thanked him and said good night.

When he had gone, she poured the coffee. She put it aside at her first sip. It was bitter. *Bitter*.

She left it on the tray.

But she kept looking at it. And later, in gown and robe, she tasted it again. *Bitter*. She hadn't imagined the foul taste. Clyde then? Budgie? Terrence when he put the flower near it?

She asked herself, if she were poisoned wouldn't everyone know?

She left the coffee in the Meissen cup, and retreated to huddle in the easy chair.

The fire burned down to glowing embers.

Could she, somewhere, somehow, sometime, have lost her mind? Wouldn't she know? Had her mother known?

Megan shivered.

She might have imagined the tiptoeing steps, the wisps of tape and thread on the tray. She might have imagined that the coffee was too bitter.

But her father had died, and Bob and Rory . . . that was the curse of Carnaby.

She was never to know love, never . . . never . . .

She knew suddenly that she had been sleeping. She knew that a sound awakened her.

She cried, "Who's there?"

Kristine came from behind the chair, hugging a pillow. "Honestly, Megan, what's wrong with you? I just wanted to say good night."

Megan smiled. "It's late, isn't it?"

"Not terribly." Kristine sat down, leaned against Megan's legs, plucked absently at the green chiffon gown, "I wanted to ask you . . . is thirteen years too big a difference between a man and a woman?"

"It depends on what man and what woman," Megan said carefully, suppressing a smile.

"But you know. Liam and me."

Kristine's wide eyes stared up at Megan.

Megan took a deep breath. "Kristine, I

don't want you to get hurt."

Kristine rocked back, no longer touching Megan. "You want him for yourself!"

Megan said coldly, "When you say such things you sound like a child, a child not old enough to be in love."

"But you do."

"You know better."

"Then why . . ."

Megan hesitated, "Liam has his reasons for being here. When he is finished with them, he'll leave. You won't ever see him again. None of us will see him again."

"What reasons?"

"I don't know them. I just know they exist."

Kristine jumped to her feet. "You just made that up, Megan."

"I'm sorry. But it's true."

Kristine ran to the door, paused there to say, "I don't believe you," and then rushed out. But moments later, she was back. She hurled herself into Megan's arms. "I'm sorry," she sobbed. "I didn't mean it, Megan. Really, I didn't."

Later Megan went to the window. She wished that she had known a better way, more kind way, of telling Kristine what must be the truth, of protecting her from the hurt of what was to come.

There was a layer of condensation on the

glass. She brushed it aside and peered out.

A downstairs light threw a faint glimmer on the slope below. Liam stood there with his hands in his pockets, looking up at the house.

Chapter 13

"You didn't drink your coffee last night," Budgie said in a voice heavy with accusation.

Megan's heart gave a frightened little quiver, but she answered, "It was too bitter."

"Espresso is supposed to be." Budgie's eyes were full of accusation.

But Megan grinned. Espresso! Not poison.

"Oh, Budgie, I'm sorry. I just didn't want it."

"Then why didn't you send it down with Clyde?"

Megan wondered, her grin fading, why Budgie was pressing the point so.

"It's not like there was anything wrong with it. I know. I fixed it myself." Budgie turned and marched out, her shoulders board stiff under her usual black silk dress.

Megan, taken aback, had not answered. She hadn't known what to say. She could hardly explain that she suspected Budgie and Clyde along with everyone in the house of wanting to kill her.

Angry, offended, or guilty, Budgie met Megan a few minutes later in the hallway, and said, "Kristine's gone down," and then walked along beside Megan to the dining room.

Kristine, in blue jeans and a heavy ski sweater, was having coffee. Liam was with her.

Megan knew that the previous night's scene hadn't been forgotten when Kristine gave her a sullen look, mumbled good morning, and turned quickly back to Liam.

"Liam," she asked, "are you going to Stoneleigh Village today? Will you let me ride along with you?"

"If I were going, I would. But I plan to stay here." He answered indulgently, as if she were a child, asking for one piece too many of candy.

Kristine noticed that, too. Her amber eyes went blank. A pink flush rose in her cheeks. "Maybe I shouldn't have asked."

He answered absently, his dark eyes slanting toward where Megan had taken a chair. "Why not, Kristine?" And then, before she could say anything, "And how are you, Megan?"

She managed an acknowledgment, avoiding his eyes, and concentrating on toast and butter.

Terrence and Celia, up earlier than usual, walked into strained silence.

"And how's your bump today, darling?" Terrence asked.

Megan said she was better, wishing that he

would stop calling her 'darling', stop giving her fond looks that she didn't want.

Then, looking at Liam, the fond look faded, the pale blue eyes narrowed. Terrence went on, "And what about you, Liam?"

Megan wondered if Liam had noticed the grudging note in the question.

Apparently, he had. A faint grin softened his mouth momentarily. He said that he was fine, adding, "I hope you don't mind that I invited myself for coffee. I guess soon you'll have to charge me board as well as rent."

But Celia's self-indulgent mouth spread with a wide grin. "It's our pleasure, believe me." She turned her head and Megan saw the chill in Celia's narrowed blue eyes as she added, "Isn't it, Megan?"

Kristine. Terrence. Celia. And Liam.

Megan wished him far away at that moment.

She wished herself far away.

Again a faint grin softened his mouth. "Megan doesn't think so!"

Celia laughed. "Oh, Liam, you don't understand."

Megan said softly, "I think he does."

"Why darling," Celia cried. "You sound hardly older than our sweetie, Kristine. You mustn't be rude to my guests."

Kristine made a small angry sound.

But Megan was silent. It was as if Vivian

had spoken through Celia. Vivian, who had hated Megan's mother, and hated her. And had always felt that the money she inherited should have belonged to Vivian herself and to Vivian's children.

Carnaby House was a giant spider spinning a web. Its fine threads and unseen threads seemed to grow tighter.

Megan sat very still, waiting.

Liam said, "This must have been a gay house in the old days with four children growing up together."

Megan finished her coffee and excused herself, and left them to it. Let them talk about the old days with Liam. She didn't want to hear them or to think about it.

She looked up at the copper tray. Clyde had re-hung it, covering the faded spot on the wall. The broken teak table was gone. There was nothing to show for that moment of terror except a tender spot on her neck, her ever-present fear.

"Can I get you something, Megan?" Clyde asked, looming suddenly in the doorway.

"Nothing, Clyde. Thanks."

"You don't have to worry about that thing anymore."

"I was just looking at it," she said quickly.

"How long are you planning to stay on, Megan?"

How long? she asked herself. However long it took. She was waiting. Waiting for whatever must happen to be over and done. She realized suddenly what that meant. She was waiting for death.

"I'm not sure, Clyde," she said finally.

Clyde lingered until Budgie came and sat down with her knitting, and made the needles flash while her sharp gray eyes watched Megan.

Chapter 14

In the two gray days that followed, indoor days with smoky fog hanging over Satan's Puddle, Megan had scarcely a moment alone. When Budgie left her, Clyde came. When Clyde had a chore, then Budgie came.

The others, Kristine, Terrence, Celia, Liam, drifted in, paused to make conversation and drifted away again.

Megan felt observed, imprisoned, threatened.

The spider tightened its web.

One night after dinner she watched the sky from the drawing room window. There were thick and scudding clouds, soft floating mists, a faint quarter of early moon.

Celia said, "Megan dear, do you know? I think you've offended Liam. I asked him to come for dinner tonight. And he said, 'No, thanks. I think not.' "

Megan turned and shrugged.

Celia's triangular smile widened. "If we want him here, we must persuade you to be nicer to him."

"I don't want him here," Megan retorted.

Kristine burst out, "But what about me?"

"No temper tantrums," Terrence told her. "It's just not your turn yet, Kristine."

"But she's had her turn," Kristine cried. "What about Bob? What about Rory?"

"That will do, children," Budgie put in firmly, sounding as if they were all five years old and quarreling over a rag doll.

Megan knew that she should laugh. But there was no laughter in her. She said, "I'm going for a walk."

Kristine wailed, "I'm sorry, Megan. I didn't mean it!"

"All right," Megan answered shortly. She stormed into the hallway, grabbed her coat, and stumbled into the thick cold air.

The scudding clouds had drawn together, but thin moonlight spilled through and turned the eaves and balustrades to silver, speckled the stone steps, glinted in the leafless trees. The wind blew. It swooped around the house, lifting Megan's hair, ripping at her coat, bringing with it a thickening mist.

Above her in Kristine's room, a light flashed on. The hot, bursting drums beat wild rhythms into the silence of the night.

Megan went down the steps. The silvering moon was gone. It was suddenly hard to see, hard to breathe.

She stumbled, following the path that wound around the house. One turn wasn't enough. She made another, then another.

Imperceptibly the wind died. The moving mist settled, thick, white, blinding.

The hot, bursting rhythm of the drums seemed muffled. The light in Kristine's room seemed dim. Carnaby House, withdrawn into a shroud of white, brooded on its ridge.

Megan paused, waited.

Somewhere near her, somewhere close, she heard a rustle of movement, a whisper of sound that drifted to her under the muffled beat of the frenetic drums.

She peered into the thick white curtain. "Who is that?"

No one answered.

The rustle of movement ceased.

She stepped off the path, eased sideways, shifting her position as quietly as she could. She held her breath, listening. There was a faint movement again. That time she was sure of it. "Who is there?" she whispered.

Again no one answered.

Yet she knew that eyes watched her, hands reached for her. She slid sideways in a few quick steps. Her heart pounded. Her ears strained to listen. Her eyes sought openings in the blinding white that surrounded her.

She staggered into something hard, cold, and froze there, hands gripping rough bark. She held her breath, listening again.

Faintly, from far away now, the drum beat drifted on the damp solid air.

She looked up at the blurred outlines of the house, the dim lights, surprised to see how far down the slope, how far from the path, she had come. As she watched the wind blew again, and the house, its diffuse lights, seemed to melt away into a distant emptiness.

When the wind died, silence fell, silence touched with the faraway sound of drums. She started up the slope, then froze again.

She heard a shuffle of footsteps, distinct, deliberate.

Someone hidden in the fog lurked between her and the house.

"Who is it?" she whispered once more, knowing that there would be no reply.

"Liam?" she asked hoarsely. "Liam, is that you?" Then, "Celia? Terrence? Are you there?" And then, in anguish, "Budgie, Clyde? Kristine? Answer me. Somebody, answer me!"

Her heart took up the rhythm of the faraway drums. Her breath became a thin gasp in her throat. Her slim, frail body became determined muscle. It was a matter of escape, survival.

She knew she must move like a shadow, like the shadow before her. She must slip away through the sheltering fog to find light and people and safety.

The copper tray had fallen, but not killed her.

She had waited, waited for this moment.

She dropped back, crept down the slope. Slowly, carefully, she began to circle the ridge.

There were no more distinct, deliberate sounds. She heard nothing. But she sensed swift, silent movement before her. Always before her. Stalking her, yet remaining always between her and the house.

She shifted, angled, changed direction, but the swift, silent movement managed always to turn her, press her, shepherd her away.

She sensed, like any small frightened thing flushed from cover, that the hunter was near, very near.

Panic flung a noose around her, flung her this way and that in an indecisive dance. Then she spun away, stumbling blindly, lost and no longer caring.

She ran, and someone ran behind her.

Then the smooth grass of Clyde's well-tended lawns became rough, slippery. Rocks slowed her, tripped her.

She fell heavily to hands and knees, and rested there, gasping, her breath a white plume instantly gone in the mist.

The noose of panic melted slowly.

She pushed herself up painfully, hands

bloodied, knees torn.

A slight breeze touched her hot cheeks, tousled her bronze curls.

She raised her head. The lights of Carnaby shone dimly on the ridge. Above them, the thick overcast had developed cracks through which narrow strips of sky showed dark.

Faintly, again, she heard the wild rhythm of the drums.

She heard the drums, and those in Carnaby would hear them, too, but loud, deafening.

Her screams would be nothing but spent breath. Spent breath, and a signal to the evil lurking in the mist.

Closer than the drums, much closer, from just below where she stood, there was the whisper of rippling water.

She clutched her coat around her, shivering, understanding, at last, that she had been dogged, driven, tracked there deliberately.

She braced herself on the bluffs above Satan's Puddle, and waited. Waited for what she knew must come.

There were long moments of silence. She stared, wide-eyed, into the blinding white emptiness.

Then she heard a sudden scraping, a clatter. She jerked sideways as a rock spun past her face. The single rock was followed by a barrage, blow after blow.

She sank under them, blood in her eyes and in her mouth.

She fell, dazed with pain, into whispering shadows.

But the whispering shadows brightened almost instantly.

Her alerted senses warned her. She heard the swift slithering movement near her, heard it while the barrage of rock continued, rained down, spun past her, clattered away in faint echoes.

She knew the touch when it came. "Liam! Not you, Liam!" she whispered.

"Hush, Megan, please." His lips were at her ear. His hand, warm and hard, pressed her mouth. His body covered hers, wide shoulders sheltering her from the spinning rocks, arms folded over her head. "Hush," he breathed.

She trembled under his weight, and felt him ease himself aside.

Their hearts seemed to beat together, always together amid the clatter of the falling stones.

The hard cold kernel of fear in her chest melted into a peculiar joy. But there was no time for understanding.

The barrage of stones came to an abrupt end. Silence fell, a dull, thick silence.

Megan waited, breathed as Liam breathed,

and then, from within the tent of silence, there was a small faint sound.

Liam's body, covering hers still, grew tense. He unfolded his arms.

She raised her head and felt sudden wind on her bloodied cheeks. She saw the mists thin and sway.

Chapter 15

The small swift sounds came closer, approaching more and more surely as the wind blew harder and the fog broke into drifting ribbons, and a sudden rim of emerging moon spread silver light. Silver light that glinted on long shining hair, and shone in wide amber eyes, and made grotesque shadows of clawed reaching hands.

Kristine.

Kristine, crawling, hands clawed and reaching, to thrust Megan over the bluffs, to send her spinning forever into Satan's Puddle.

Kristine, crawling through fog, now wrapped in silver moonlight, wide eyes staring, straining, through the bright veil of her hair.

The moment of recognition seemed to last a lifetime.

But Megan was suddenly free.

Kristine rose, and Liam flung himself at her in a low flat dive that caught her as she spun away, and held her, and set her on her feet still holding her.

The wind had blown all their whispered cries away. But now it died.

In the vast and empty silence, Megan got up.

Kristine, leaning against Liam, cried, "Megan, what happened? I heard you running, and called you, and tried to come after you. But you wouldn't listen to me. You wouldn't stop. And I heard all that noise, and couldn't understand. What happened, Megan?"

Megan's lips were stiff, cold. She couldn't answer. Horror held her as firmly as Liam held Kristine.

He said, "Kristine, Kristine, we know."

"You know?" Kristine's expressionless eyes sought Megan's bloodied face. "You know what? I was just coming after you to apologize again, Megan. That was awful of me. To say that. About you having had your chance. I'm sorry. Truly I am."

"Are you sorry for what you've done?" Liam asked gently. "Can you think of it at all?"

Megan, staring into Kristine's eyes, stumbled forward.

Liam shook his head.

She paused, and Kristine cried, "But I haven't done anything."

Liam's dark somber gaze shifted to Megan. He said deliberately, "I'm going to marry your sister, Kristine."

Megan gasped, "No. No."

But Kristine screamed, twisted and writhed in Liam's grasp. "You can't," she screamed. "You belong to me!"

"Is that what you told Rory, Kristine? And did he laugh at you? Is that why you shot him?"

She gave Liam a sly look. "You think you know it all. But you're wrong. That was for Megan. We were supposed to have our dresses fitted. I called there, left word for Megan that I was going to the movies. But I went to Rory's instead. He had those silly guns of his on his desk. I asked him to show me how they get loaded. And he did. So I hugged him. And I took the gun and pushed it against his chest, and when it fired, he fell down. After that, I went to the movies." She added, to Megan, "But it was for you, Megan. I didn't want Rory. I wanted you. For myself."

Megan wavered on her feet, small hands clenched at her torn lips. Kristine, sweet, adoring Kristine . . .

"And Bob, Kristine?" Liam asked. "You were ten then, a long time ago. Do you remember Bob?"

She answered, her voice light, young, but dull, as if hypnotized by memory. "Oh, yes, I remember Bob. You were going to run away with him, Megan. I heard you plan it all. And that day I went down to see the shell he'd found. I got on the boat with him. He had that spare oar. I hit him on the head, hard, very hard. He fell into the lake. And all I had to do was push the boat off. The wind took it away."

She didn't know what she sounded like, Megan thought. Kristine didn't understand the mad, terrible words that poured out of her lips.

Megan whispered, "Enough, Kristine."

But Kristine went on, as though once started, she was unable to stop. "Don't you remember Daddy, Megan? The trip that I couldn't go on? He was going to take you away from me, wasn't he? We were going for a walk that night. He waited for me outside. I got the vase. I stood above him there on the steps, I hit him and he fell down, and then I hit him again, and the vase broke. He cried out my name, but I left him. Remember, Megan, how he kept saying my name until he died the next day?"

Megan remembered. He had called for Kristine. Not for Megan. Yes, she remembered that well.

"You belonged to me, Megan," Kristine continued. "But I didn't know how it would be to grow up. How it would be to know Liam and want him. But he liked you. Not Celia.

Not me. Just you, Megan."

"The tray," Liam said softly.

Kristine nodded. "Yes, but it missed. So I waited, and waited. But there was no chance, not until tonight. Megan got mad at me and went outside. I went up to my room. I set the LP record going. My drums . . . They make so much noise."

"Kristine, oh, Kristine," Megan gasped. The paralysis of horror which had held her seemed to melt away. Though Liam shook his head at her, she stumbled toward them.

Kristine cried, "I'm sorry, Megan. Oh, I'm so sorry," her face suddenly wet with tears. "Forgive me. Please forgive me, Megan."

Automatically, Megan reached for her as she had done so many times before. She opened her arms and took Kristine from Liam, and for an instant, Kristine lay against her, leaned on her, hugged her. And then Kristine was gone.

Fleet as the wind, with the wind itself, she was gone from Megan's arms, gone from between Megan and Liam.

Kristine ran, just inches beyond Megan's reaching fingertips, beyond Liam's grasping hands.

She ran to the edge of the bluff, hung there for an endless instant, then disappeared.

Later, white-faced Budgie explained that

Clyde had found the wisps of tape, shreds of cord on the tray, and knew someone had tried to kill Megan. They set themselves to watch over her, not knowing if she had guessed. Celia, bright smile gone, cried, "But she went up to her room. That wild music . . ." And Clyde, nodding nervously told her, "It's what fooled us, Celia. The music." Terrence just shook his blond head.

But that was later.

At that moment, standing on the edge of the bluff when Kristine disappeared in a clatter of terrible sounds, Megan felt that she must follow Kristine to Satan's Puddle, to death.

But Liam took her into his arms. "I'm sorry, Megan."

She shook her head, leaning against his strength. Once again she felt a peculiar joy at his touch. Now she understood it. Now she was willing to understand it. "Poor Kristine. The curse of Carnaby . . . and all these years Liam, I thought that anyone I loved had to die."

"It's over, Megan."

She looked at him. The peculiar joy she felt at his touch was love, known since that first night in the fog. And her fear of him had been fear of love, fear of the Carnaby curse. Not of Liam. Never of Liam.

He bent his head. The moonlight was on his face.

She saw the quick familiar look, and that time she recognized it. She gasped, "Rory!"

"Rory's brother, Megan. The one you never met because he was overseas." Liam grinned. "Well, I never lied to you. I *was* overseas in Viet Nam, as a correspondent. When I heard what happened, I just couldn't believe it. It wasn't Rory's style. So I checked with the police. They'd closed it out as suicide. I did some thinking and checked you out. Though I never saw you. I found that your father had died suddenly. A childhood sweetheart had died suddenly. And then there was Rory."

"And you thought that . . . that I . . . ?"

"I thought I wanted to know you. It was convenient that the Parrs brought you here. I got hold of the Johnstones as soon as I heard that. They passed me on, so here I came, right after you. But when I saw you, I knew . . . I knew you were no triple murderess, no more than Rory was a suicide. Then that business with the copper tray. It scared me and confused me. I tried the hat on the Parrs, on Budgie and Clyde. Finally, I began to consider Kristine. I watched you, and I watched her. And neither of you made it easy. I was outside tonight, like every night. You came out, and I followed you. I stayed with you the whole time, hoping she'd show herself." His voice went very deep. "She did."

Megan, still within the circle of his arms, moved to look toward Satan's Puddle. But he turned her away from it.

"No," he said. "Don't look back. Look ahead. To the future. Remember, Megan. I've already said I'm going to marry you."

"Look ahead," she repeated, and smiled at him.

Together they climbed the slope to the suddenly bright lights of Carnaby House.

The employees of THORNDIKE PRESS hope you have enjoyed this Large Print book. All our Large Print titles are designed for easy reading, and all our books are made to last. Other Thorndike Large Print books are available at your library, through selected bookstores, or directly from us. For more information about current and upcoming titles, please call or mail your name and address to: